ABRAHAM

This edition is dedicated to the memory of
Dr ALAN BRYNE REYNOLDS (1910-1991),
Warden of Churchill Hall (1956-1972), and
Lecturer in English (1947-1975), University of Bristol.

ABRAHAM COWLEY

Selected Poems

*Edited with an Introduction and Notes
by David Hopkins and Tom Mason*

Fyfield Books

First published in 1994 by
Carcanet Press Limited
402-406 Corn Exchange Buildings
Manchester M4 3BY

Selection, introduction and notes
Copyright © David Hopkins and Tom Mason 1994

A CIP catalogue record for this book
is available from the British Library.
ISBN 1 85754 119 7

The publisher acknowledges financial assistance
from the Arts Council of England

Set in 10pt Palatino by Bryan Williamson, Frome
Printed and bound in England by SRP Ltd, Exeter

Funded by
THE
ARTS
COUNCIL
OF ENGLAND

Contents

Acknowledgements

We are grateful to the University of Bristol Alumni Foundation and the Winston Churchill Birthday Foundation for grants towards the publication costs of this volume, to Sandra Hopkins for assistance in checking texts, and to Dr Paul Hammond for his helpful comments on our manuscript.

Principal Dates in Cowley's Life

1618 Born in London, the posthumous seventh son of Thomas Cowley, stationer.

before 1628 Reads Spenser's *Faerie Queene*. Later attributes to this experience his decision to embark on a poetic career.

?1628-36 At Westminster School (King's Scholar, 1630).

1633 First volume, *Poetical Blossoms*, published (expanded edition, with new section, *Sylva*, 1636; third edition, 1637).

1636-43 At Trinity College, Cambridge (Scholar, 1637; BA, 1639; Minor Fellow, 1640; MA, 1642). During this period makes the acquaintance of Richard Crashaw, William Hervey, and Lucius Carey, Viscount Falkland.

1639 Latin comedy, *Naufragium Joculare* ('The Laughable Shipwreck'), performed at Trinity College.

1642 12 March: Comedy, *The Guardian*, played before the twelve-year-old Prince Charles at Trinity College.

Publication of *The Puritan's Lecture*, a satire on Puritan preachers.

1643 In response to the growing Puritan influence in Cambridge, moves to St John's College, Oxford. During this period, visits Falkland at Great Tew. William Harvey performing medical researches in Oxford at this time.

Publication of *The Puritan and the Papist*, a savage satire on religious extremism.

Writes *The Civil War*, an epic poem on recent events (abandoned, late 1643; Book 1 published, 1679; Books 2-3 published from manuscript, 1973).

1644-54 Based in France, in the service of Lord Jermyn, secretary to Queen Henrietta Maria. Employed on ciphering and intelligence work and on royalist missions to the Netherlands, Scotland and Jersey. Meets Thomas Hobbes, William Davenant, Edmund Waller and Crashaw in France during this period.

1647 Unauthorised publication in London of *The Mistress* (a collection of love-poems).

1649 Before 25 August: Death of Crashaw at Loreto, Italy.

1650 Publication of *The Guardian*.

1654	August-September: Cowley returns to England. Suspected by some royalists of involvement in secret dealings between the Duke of Buckingham and Cromwell.
1655	12 April: Arrested in London with other suspected royalists, and imprisoned. Released on the bail of the physician, Dr Charles Scarborough, an old Cambridge friend, and lives in England until 1659. During this period, makes acquaintance of Katherine Philips and Thomas Sprat.
1656	Collected, authorized, folio edition of Cowley's *Poems* published. Comprises Preface, *Miscellanies* (occasional poems and translations), a reprint of *The Mistress, Pindaric Odes* (in imitation and emulation of the Greek poet, Pindar), and the *Davideis* (an unfinished biblical epic, of which four books of the projected twelve were completed).
1657	Created Doctor of Physic by Oxford University, after a period of private medical studies in Kent. 15 September: Celebrates the marriage of the newly-returned Buckingham to the daughter of Thomas, Lord Fairfax.
1659-60	Returns to France. Accepted back into Jermyn's service.
1660	Publication of *Ode, upon the Blessed Restoration and Return of ...Charles the Second*.
1661	January: Reinstated to his Trinity Fellowship. Publication of *A Proposition for the Advancement of Experimental Philosophy* (a plan for a neo-Baconian 'philosophical college'). 16 December: *Cutter of Coleman-Street* (comedy) performed (published, 1663). Disappointed at not being appointed to the sinecure post of Master of the Savoy, promised him before the Restoration. Publication of *The Visions and Prophecies Concerning England, Scotland and Ireland, of Ezekiel Grebner* (a satire on Cromwell, re-issued with different titles later the same year, and in the 1668 *Works*).
1662	Given the leasehold of land in Kent, for services rendered to Queen Henrietta Maria. Publication of *Plantarum Libri Duo* (a Latin poem on the properties of herbs).
1663	Retires to Barn Elms in Surrey.

Publication of *Verses Written upon Several Occasions* (miscellaneous poems written since 1656).

November-December: Seriously ill with a fever.

Passed over again for the Mastership of the Savoy.

1663-4   Works on *Plantarum Libri III-IV* (on flowers; published in *Poemata Latina*, 1668).

1665   Moves to Chertsey, where he lives in retirement as a gentleman-farmer. During this period works on *Plantarum Libri V-VI* (on fruit trees of the Old and New Worlds, and the greatness of the English nation; published in *Poemata Latina*, 1668), and on *Several Discourses by way of Essays in Verse and Prose*, reflections on retirement and tranquillity of the soul (published in *Works*, 1668; incorporates some translations published in the 1663 *Verses*).

1667   Publication of the Ode 'To the Royal Society' in Thomas Sprat's *History of the Royal Society*.

28 July: Dies of pneumonia.

3 August: Buried in Westminster Abbey, next to Chaucer and Spenser.

1668   Publication of *The Works of Mr Abraham Cowley*, edited by Sprat (the 1656 collection, plus the 1663 *Verses* with additions, the *Essays*, and the two prose pamphlets of 1661). Contains Sprat's 'Account of the Life and Writings of Mr Abraham Cowley'.

Publication of *Poemata Latina*, also edited by Sprat. Contains Sprat's shorter Latin account of Cowley's life and writings.

Introduction: The Pleasures of Cowley

Abraham Cowley, who was Milton's favourite contemporary poet and Dryden's acknowledged 'master', and who was admired by Rochester, Pope, Johnson, Cowper and Wordsworth,[1] is nowadays a largely neglected figure, known to general readers only by mostly unflattering hearsay, or by a few, often unrepresentative, anthology pieces. The present volume is designed to present and annotate some of his best poems in a way that might assist modern readers to recapture some of the pleasures which Cowley's verse gave to so many for so long.

Part of the difficulty of introducing Cowley to new readers is one of characterization and definition. It is not easy to say what *kind* of poet he was. His poems do not seem to have the idiosyncrasy and drama of Donne's, the purity and moral weight of some of Ben Jonson's, the coolness or intricacy of Marvell's, or the energy and perspicacity of some of Dryden's. Cowley has been described both as a 'decadent-metaphysical' and a 'proto-Augustan' poet, but, on closer inspection, neither epithet really seems to fit the vast majority of his poems. Cowley himself wrote a great deal about poetry, but his remarks hardly amount to any kind of manifesto or self-definition.

It is probably no accident that the most frequently-remembered criticism of Cowley has come from the hand of Samuel Johnson in his *Lives of the Poets* (1779-81),[2] and one of the major purposes of the present Introduction is to elucidate some of the implications of Johnson's classic account, the assumptions and idiom of which can sometimes seem rather unfamiliar and offputting to the modern reader. Johnson's peculiar qualification as a critic of Cowley was his ability to rest easily within contradictory statements. For it appears to be the case that, in the interests of accuracy and truth, every descriptive remark about Cowley's poetry needs to be balanced by an equal and opposite comment. Thus, if we say, 'Cowley's poetry is difficult', which is obviously true, we need to balance the judgement with the equally correct proposition, 'Cowley's poetry is noticeably easy'. When we say, with Johnson, 'if Cowley has a good line, he has it by chance', we have also to follow Johnson in his observation that 'Cowley has left unsurpassed examples of representative versification' [i.e. verse in which rhythm and movement act almost like imagery, and render the sense to perfection]. If we claim that Cowley is persistently 'classical', we also have to say that he was the most innovative poet of his generation. If we class Cowley among the most varied of poets, we must at the same time notice the presence of a number of simple, determining, all-pervading ideas. Cowley's ambition, it must be observed, is equally matched by his modesty; his lightness and wit are equally matched by his ardour and thoughtfulness.

Cowley's poems, it is clear, were appreciated by his first readers for all these qualities. Johnson noticed the 'great variety of style and sentiment, from burlesque levity to awful [i.e. awe-inspiring] grandeur' offered by Cowley's *Miscellanies*, and remarked that 'such an assemblage of diversified excellence no other poet has hitherto afforded'. During his own lifetime and for fifty years after his death, Cowley's poems seem to have been read more widely and with more general admiration than Ben Jonson's, Donne's, or Marvell's. Dryden was thought to have surpassed, but not to have eclipsed, Cowley, and many of Cowley's poems survived well beyond the hundred years traditionally set as the test of art. As late as 1893 the critic A.H. Bullen could simply assume that all educated readers would have 'The Grasshopper' by heart.[3] And Cowley's *Essays in Verse and Prose* were in print, in several popular editions, until well into the present century.

It is particularly striking to find a poet now thought of, if at all, as the author of extravagant 'metaphysical' conceits being praised for his 'ease'. The term 'easy poetry' was employed most famously and cogently by Johnson in No. 77 of *The Idler*. There he observed that 'Cowley seems to have possessed the power of writing easily beyond any other of our poets'. 'Easy poetry' is defined by Johnson as 'that in which natural thoughts are expressed without violence to the language'. Johnson equates violence with artifice: 'Where any artifice appears in the construction of the verse, that verse is no longer easy'. Violence is done to language 'by harsh or daring figures, by transposition, by unusual acceptations [i.e. meanings] of words, and by any licence which would be avoided by a writer of prose'. Johnson took care to distinguish the diction of 'easy' poetry from that of *colloquial* poetry, poetry which adopts the exact speech of its day, including mannerisms, slang, and fashionable jargon – 'modes of speech which owe their prevalance only to modish folly, or the eminence of those that use them'.

Johnson returned to these thoughts in his 'Life of Cowley' when discussing Cowley's versions of some poems attributed to the Greek poet, Anacreon – poems in praise of love and wine, where the very 'morality is voluptuous'. 'Levity of thought', wrote Johnson, 'naturally produced familiarity of language, and the familiar part of language continues long the same: the dialogue of comedy when it is transcribed from popular manners and real life, is read from age to age with equal pleasure':

> The *Anacreontics*, therefore, of Cowley give now all the pleasure which they ever gave. If he was formed by nature for one kind of writing more than another, his power seems to have been greatest in the familiar and the festive.

As far as any descriptive terms characterize Cowley adequately, 'familiar' and 'festive' would seem to be among the most useful. The prevailing tone of almost all his poems is intimate and light. This tone is most pure in the *Anacreontics* which begin the present selection, but it is also obvious in Cowley's many poems of friendly address. The reader is assumed to be a close acquaintance, like-minded, affable. Cowley's poems are offered as if to a friend for that friend's delight. He tenders advice, makes moral points, but never moralizes or preaches. He is often chatty, but never merely modish or slangy.

What may seem strange is that this familiar, smiling manner is also the ground tone of the ambitious and elaborate Odes which Cowley wrote in imitation of the Greek poet, Pindar, and even, at times, of his attempt to write a religious epic, the *Davideis*. There are excursions into other registers, but almost every poem returns, ultimately, to 'the familiar and the festive'. Cowley's diction remains familiar even when the subject-matter treats topics which would seem to demand the most elevated or serious language, such as the speech of a god, the troubles of David and

Jonathan, or the Civil War. Cowley is never entirely solemn – if solemnity requires the suppression of all sideways movements of mind, and of every hint or suspicion of laughter.

Cowley's very versification seems designed to create an effect of familiarity. Sometimes this means that his lines flow with an effortless mellifluousness which makes them, as it were, 'read themselves'. But elsewhere Cowley's striving after an effect of natural 'ease' has, paradoxically, caused a number of problems for his readers. While Milton appears sometimes to have been trying to persuade the texture of his English to imitate that of Latin or Greek, Cowley seems to have wanted his verse to dance the dance of excited speech. As a result, to modern – as, indeed, to many eighteenth-century – ears, his poems often seem full of metrical stumbling-blocks. Indeed, he seems to have been well aware that he was presenting problems and challenges to his readers – in his Odes particularly, which mingle long and short lines, and lines that are predominately iambic with others that are trochaic or even anapaestic.

A particular feature of Cowley's versification which is likely to give readers trouble (as it did the editors of this volume: see 'A Note on Texts') is the poet's habit of eliding syllables. This goes well beyond the normal conventions of the seventeenth century, whether in prose or verse. Where it has been habitual since the middle of the nineteenth century to pronounce every syllable when reciting verse, 'mouthing out', as Tennyson puts it, the 'oes and aes' to create 'deep-chested music', Cowley seems to have made the opposite assumption : that in excited speech, the power of the iambic line would lead to the swallowing of unneccessary syllables and the running of words into one another. Particular difficulty in this respect will perhaps be found when Cowley elides his rhyme words – 'refine't/ coin't' (for 'refine it/ coin it'); 'by't/ sight' (for 'by it/ sight').

The manner of Cowley's poems, by generally avoiding some of the usual stylistic devices which mark off verse from prose, may deserve to be called 'easy', but its matter is consistently of a kind which could not be presented in prose. The distinction between Cowley's prose and his poetry is not one which depends on vocabulary or word-order or versification, but on *thought*. Poetry, it seems, was, for Cowley, a medium for saying precisely that which could not be said in prose. For some eighteenth-century readers, Cowley's combination of hard thoughts in easy language was unpalatable. Cowley's editor, Bishop Richard Hurd, for example, thought that

> Mr Cowley's poetry . . . is often much disfigured by the double affectation of wit and familiarity. He would say an out-of-the-way thing, in a trival manner. But such was the court idea, in his time, of writing like a gentleman.[4]

The difficulty was thought to lie in the presence within a largely plain and familiar diction and apparently casual versification of the conspicuously far-sought and hard-laboured. Surprise – the unusual word carefully placed, a sudden reference to an object, phenomenon, or body of thought outside the apparent decorum of the poem – seems to have been what Cowley wanted from poetry, and almost always provided. He seems to have particularly enjoyed playing with 'philosophies', and making sudden transitions between different levels of seriousness.

Judging from his manuscripts, and from the early printed texts of his poems (many of which were authorially supervised, and which employ italicisation to a degree and in a manner beyond that which was normal in the period), it looks as if Cowley wanted some of his words to be given an unusual kind of emphasis – a smile of special consideration, as it were. One such word, an extreme example of his deployment of 'out-of-the-way' terms, is *'antiperistasis'* in the 'Elegy upon Anacreon', where Cowley praises the Greek poet for continuing to love and drink and dance in extreme old age: 'Th' *antiperístasis* of age / More inflamed thy am'orous rage.' In his *Dictionary*, Johnson, citing these lines, took nearly a hundred words to explain Cowley's surprise word:

> *Antiperistasis*: The opposition of a contrary quality, by which the quality it opposes becomes heightened or intended [i.e. made intense]; or the action, by which a body attacked by another collects itself and becomes stronger by such opposition; or an intention of the activity of one quality caused by the opposition of another. Thus quicklime is set on fire by the

affusion of cold water; so water becomes warmer in winter than in summer; and thunder and lightning are excited in the middle region of the air, which is continually cold, and all by *antiperistasis*. This is an exploded principle in the Peripatetic philosophy.

The reader will decide whether or not Cowley's far-fetched application of an obscure, obsolete, Greek philosophical term to the sexual 'fires' of the aged Anacreon is a pedantic whimsy or a bold, witty stroke which is well 'worth the carriage'.

Johnson, at any rate, described the 'volatility' of the most successful of the exuberant imaginative leaps to be found in Cowley's poetry as 'not the flutter of a light [i.e. trivial], but the bound of an elastic [i.e. flexible, intellectually agile] mind', and, like Wordsworth, he was emphatic in his praise of Cowley's *sense*. In many cases he judged Cowley's extravagance to be the *expression* rather than the *evasion* of thought. Boswell reports:

> I mentioned Shenstone's saying of Pope, that he had the art of condensing sense more than anybody. Dr Johnson said, 'It is not true, Sir. There is more sense in a line of Cowley than in a page . . . of Pope'.[5]

Another example of Cowley's 'far-fetched' wit is to be found in his use of the word 'interregnum' (the period during which a throne is vacant between the death of one king or prince and the accession of another) in 'The Chronicle', one of the most enduringly popular of his poems, in which the changes in a young man's affections are compared to the vicissitudes of kingdoms as recorded by chroniclers. Here 'interregnum' probably has a specific reference to the period after the Civil War, to a set of events which, by his own account, were the worst things that ever happened to Cowley:

> With . . . my heart wholly set upon letters [i.e. a literary career], I went to the university, but was soon torn from thence by that violent public storm which would suffer nothing to stand where it did, but rooted up every plant, even from the princely cedars to me, the hyssop.

> (Essay: 'Of Myself')

In the poem, the 'interregnum' of the heart is linked to 'anarchy', itself a more disturbing and weighty word for a seventeenth-century royalist than might be immediately obvious today. Both terms, however, are presented as contributing to a kind of joke. The speaker of the poem has been giving a list of the rulers of his affections. Susanna has just been driven out by Isabella:

> But in her place I then obeyed
>   Black-eyed Bess, her viceroy-maid,
>   To whom ensued a vacancy.
> Thousand worse passions then possessed
> The interregnum of my breast;
>   Bless me from such an anarchy!

The effect of Cowley's witticism here, as of this poem as a whole, seems to be to encourage the reader to view both affairs of the heart and disturbingly painful public events, momentarily, with an amused *insouciance* and consequent sense of perspective which is seldom possible in the normal heat of living. 'The Chronicle', it is interesting to note, was a poem which Johnson considered 'unequal and alone' in revealing the strength beneath Cowley's 'volatility', judging that 'even in this airy frolic of genius', Cowley's 'levity never leaves his learning behind it; the moralist, the politician, and the critic mingle their influence'.

The thought-provoking word set amidst playfulness is deployed particularly strikingly by Cowley in a number of instances when that word is the name of a philosophical sect. On one occasion, Cowley's Anacreon makes the following plea:

> Crown me with roses whilst I live,
> Now your wines and ointments give.
> After death I nothing crave,
> Let me'alive my pleasures have;
> All are Stoics in the grave.

When writing in this vein, another favourite word of Cowley's is 'epicurean'. His version of the tale of the country mouse (see pp. 57-59) gives the town (in this case, courtly) mouse an 'epicurean mind' – where the term has its popular meaning ('given to expensive and luxurious tastes in food'). It turns out, however, that it

xix

is the country mouse who actually manifests the simple contentment recommended in the teachings of the Greek philosopher Epicurus, and who is thus the true 'Epicurean'.[6]

Cowley's grasshopper is an even more perfect embodiment of truly 'Epicurean' happiness. The challenge of 'The Grasshopper', the tenth poem in the *Anacreontics*, is to see this insect as living, perfectly naturally, a life in which the simple pleasures of existence are relished to the full, and towards which all wise human beings should therefore strive:

> To thee, of all things upon earth,
> Life is no longer than thy mirth.
> Happy insect, happy thou,
> Dost neither age nor winter know!
> But when thou'st drunk, and danced, and sung
> Thy fill, the flow'ry leaves among
> (Voluptuous, and wise withal,
> Epicurean animal!),
> Sated with thy summer feast,
> Thou retir'st to endless rest.[7]

Cowley's constant deployment of unusual words, and constant references to unfamiliar objects, phenomena, and ideas mean that notes, although kept in this edition to a minimum, are a necessary evil, if his poems are to be properly understood. They are made necessary not merely because of the passage of time, but because of Cowley's distinctive cast of mind. As Johnson remarked, Cowley 'brought to his poetic labours a mind replete with learning...His pages are embellished with all the ornaments which books could supply'. Cowley, Johnson noted, had 'a mind capacious by nature, and replenished by study', and visited 'recesses of learning not much frequented by common readers of poetry'. To some of his poems, the *Pindaric Odes* and the *Davideis*, Cowley provided notes himself. These give some idea of the kinds of resources he had at his disposal, and the kinds of expectation he was making of his readers. The list of his references is miscellaneous and large: Chaucer, Ovid, Livy, Claudian, Hippocrates, Plutarch, Porphyrius, *Genesis*, Virgil, Lucretius, Seneca, St Paul, St Jerome, Horace, Euripides, Aquinas, Macrobius,

Plato. Since Cowley does not so much borrow from these writers as imitate and transform fragments and ideas, it is not always strictly necessary to know his 'source' in order to appreciate his broad imaginative drift. But sometimes the assimilation and transformation is less complete, and the reader is thus at a loss without some knowledge of the materials on which Cowley's mind was working. Moreover, a knowledge of Cowley's source sometimes allows the reader to appreciate a learned allusion which, in the poet's hands, operates almost like a joke.

Cowley's characteristic use of his recondite learning can be seen to advantage in 'The Muse', one of the *Pindaric Odes* in which he attempts to define and praise the idea of poetry. Cowley begins – alluding *en route* to Pindar, Porphyrius, *Genesis*, Virgil, Lucretius and Ovid – by evoking the power of poetry to create entities and phenomena outside the normal course of nature, and by suggesting that the poet's creative capacities might thus be considered as more extensive than those of God himself. Then, having described, with allusions to ancient astrological belief and to Seneca, the power of poetry over matter and over past and future time, he finally turns to poetry's dealings with eternity:

> Thou stop'st this current, and dost make
> This running river settle like a lake;
> Thy certain hand holds fast this slipp'ry snake.

Johnson observed that Cowley characteristically provides 'inferences rather than images, and shows not what may be supposed to have been seen, but what *thoughts* the sight might have *suggested*' [our italics]. In the lines just quoted, nothing is done to encourage a reader to visualize the snake. The point, as Cowley's notes make clear, is partly the difficulty of holding such a creature fast, and partly, in the poet's mind at least, the fact that 'a snake with the tail in the mouth of it was the ancient hieroglyphic of the year'. A similar movement of mind seems to lie behind Cowley's puzzling phrase 'round eternity' a few lines later:

> Nay, thy immortal rhyme
> Makes this one short point of time
> To fill up half the orb of round eternity.

Cowley explains:

> There are two sorts of eternity; from the present backwards to eternity, and from the present forwards, called by the school-men [i.e. medieval scholastic theologians and philosophers] *aeternitas a parte ante* and *aeternitas a parte post*. These two make up the whole circuit of eternity, which the present time cuts like a diameter, but poetry makes it extend to all eternity to come, which is the half-circle.

One essential quality of 'The Muse' – that it draws on a great many works of literature and large bodies of thought without resembling or simply endorsing any of them – became part of the standard praise of Cowley: 'To him no author was unknown; / Yet what he writ was all his own.' These lines, by Cowley's friend, Sir John Denham,[8] were commended by Johnson, who remarked that 'this wide position requires less limitation when it is affirmed of Cowley than perhaps of any other poet; he read much and yet borrowed little'. Many of Cowley's early readers praise him for being the 'English Horace', 'English Virgil', or 'English Anacreon'. The emphasis here must fall on 'English'. Cowley's discovery was to see that it was not necessary to follow the surface features and particulars of the original Latin or Greek any more when 'translating' than when 'imitating' ancient poems. He was, observed Johnson, 'among those who freed translation from servility, and, instead of following his authors at a distance, walked by their side'.

In the Preface to his *Pindaric Odes*, Cowley wrote: 'I am not so much enamoured of the name 'translator' not to wish, rather, to be something better, though it want yet a name'. An example of what that 'something better' might be may be suggested by a comparison with Milton. Both poets attempted English versions of an Ode (1.5) in which Horace had addressed a former mistress, Pyrrha, on the subject of a young boy who had succeeded the poet in Pyrrha's affections. In his translation, Milton stuck as closely as possible to the original, and described his poem as having been 'rendered almost word for word, without rhyme, according to the Latin measure, as near as the language will permit'. His version of Horace's first stanza runs:

What slender youth, bedewed with liquid odours
Courts thee on roses in some pleasant cave;
    Pyrrha, for whom bind'st thou
    In wreaths thy golden hair,
Plain in thy neatness.

Cowley's rendering displays his customary ease, festivity, and gaiety:

    To whom now, Pyrrha, art thou kind?
      To what heart-ravished lover
    Dost thou thy golden locks unbind,
      Thy hidden sweets discover;
    And with large bounty open set
All the bright stores of thy rich cabinet?

There may, however, have been a price to pay for such unequivocal 'Englishing' of Horace's Latin. Some readers have felt that Horace and Milton place more stress than Cowley on the dangers of the situation being described. Johnson thought 'slight and trifling' Cowley's vesion of the lines in the poem in which the poet warns his successful rival of emotional storms to come. Here is Milton's rendering:

      O how oft shall he
On faith and changèd gods complain: and seas
    Rough with black winds and storms
    Unwonted shall admire;
Who now enjoys thee credulous, all gold,
Who always vacant, always amiable
    Hope thee; of flattering gales
    Unmindful?

Cowley transposes the lines to a recognisably English setting:

    He'enjoys thy calmy sunshine now
      And no breath stirring hears;
    In the clear heaven of thy brow
      No smallest cloud appears.
    He sees thee gentle, fair, and gay,
    And trusts the faithless April of thy May.

Cowley was not prepared to abandon himself to the Roman poets to the same extent as Dryden. His selection of Latin poetry, and the aspects of that poetry which he chose to emphasize, are very much those which accord with his own temperament and preoccupations. It is telling, for example, that his version of Horace's Second Epode omits the ironic turn of the final lines, in which the praise of country life which had occupied the main body of the poem is suddenly revealed as the utterance of a businessman who is unwilling to leave his worldly pursuits except in his imagination. Cowley's concentration in his Latin translations is usually on a few simple thoughts – that life is safest when lived at home, and that a simple life in the country is to be preferred to the inevitable troubles of city and state. The Roman poetry he most admired seems to have offered him a vision of how a wise man might find content of mind together with particulars to give embodiment to that content. This vision is summed up neatly in the imperatives of the last four lines of his version of the forty-seventh epigram from Martial's tenth book:

> Be satisfied and pleased with what thou art;
> Act cheerfully and well th' allotted part,
> Enjoy the present hour, be thankful for the past,
> And neither fear, nor wish th' approaches of the last.

It is with Horace, however, – or, rather, with one side of Horace – that Cowley was felt by contemporaries and successors to have had the closest affinity. By Cowley's own account, a love of Horace seems to have grown in him with a love of poetry and a love of the simple life. In his essay 'Of Myself' Cowley claimed that the fundamental cast of his mind had not altered with the years: 'that I was then of the same mind as I am now (which, I confess, I wonder at myself) may appear by the latter end of an ode which I made when I was but thirteen years old'. The childhood poem referred to describes a simple and untroubled life, and ends with these lines:

> Thus would I double my life's fading space,
> For he that runs it well, twice runs his race.
>   And in this true delight,
>   These unbought sports, this happy state,

> I would not fear nor wish my fate,
> 　　But boldly say each night,
> 'Tomorrow let my sun his beams display,
> 　Or in clouds hide them; I have lived today'.

Cowley commented:

> You may see by it I was even then acquainted with the poets,
> for the conclusion is taken out of Horace; and perhaps it was
> the immature and immoderate love of them which stamped
> first, or rather engraved, these characters in me. They were
> like letters cut into the bark of a young tree, which with the tree
> still grow proportionably.

There is a sad contrast between the desires expressed in Cowley's poems for an 'Horatian' ease, and the vicissitudes of his real life, which made it impossible for him ever to say 'I have lived today'. It seems to have been in poetry, and only in poetry, that Cowley could find 'true delight' : poetry was, for him, as it were, a *place*, the only place where true happiness could be found:

> If life should a well-ordered poem be
> 　(In which he only hits the white
> Who joins true profit with the best delight),
> 　The more heroic strain let others take,
> 　　Mine the pindaric way I'll make.
> The matter should be grave, the numbers loose and free.
> 　It shall not keep one settled pace of time;
> 　In the same tune it shall not always chime,
> 　Nor shall each day just to his neighbour rhyme.
> 　A thousand liberties it shall dispense,
> 　　And manage all without offence.
> 　　　('Ode: Upon Liberty', from the essay 'Of Liberty')

It is remarkable that in this last wish, Cowley's fate matched his desires. Whatever may have been his misfortunes in the public sphere, Cowley, it seems, had no enemies in literary circles, and early responses to his work are remarkably untouched by the backbiting, resentment, and acrimony which characterise so much literary comment of his day. There are some humorous comments in his poem of self-pity, 'The Complaint', but otherwise Cowley's modesty seems to have disarmed all he met and all who read him. 'His modesty and humility were so great that if he had not had many other equal virtues, they might have been thought dissimulation', wrote his friend and biographer, Thomas Sprat: 'He had a great integrity and plainness of manners, which he preserved to the last'. Cowley's essay on himself was recommended to the young well into the nineteenth century as a classic of modesty:

> It is a hard and nice subject for a man to write of himself; it grates his own heart to say anything of disparagement, and the reader's ears to hear anything of praise from him. There is no danger from me of offending him in this kind. Neither my mind, nor my body, nor my fortune, allow me any materials for that vanity. It is sufficient for my own contentment that they have preserved me from being scandalous, or remarkable on the defective side.

In the end, the attractiveness of Cowley's poetry comes close to the attractiveness of the personality of Cowley the man, as perceived by his contemporaries. Johnson called Cowley 'the most amiable of mankind', and the same adjective, 'amiable' (a much stronger word in the eighteenth and early nineteenth centuries than it is today), was used by Wordsworth to sum up his deep affection for Cowley's poetic character. It was Cowley's 'amiability', perhaps, which made his poems of friendship, whether real or (as in 'The Country Mouse') imagined, among the most enduringly popular poems of this kind in the language.

One of the most striking of Cowley's poems of friendship, 'On the Death of Mr William Hervey', contains a couplet which combines the poet's characteristic wit (evidenced in the astrological term 'influence') with his, equally characteristic, strong and simple sentiment: 'He was my friend, the truest friend on earth; / A strong and mighty influ'ence joined our birth.' Along with 'The Chronicle' and the *Anacreontics*, Johnson picked out for special praise the 'verses upon Crashaw, which apparently [i.e. clearly, obviously] excel all that have gone before them, and in which there are beauties which common authors may justly think not only above their attainment, but above their ambition'. The poet Richard Crashaw (?1613-49) and Cowley seem to have been friends at university. Crashaw was expelled from a Fellowship at Peterhouse, Cambridge, and travelled to Paris, where he converted to the Roman Catholic church. The two men met again in France. Crashaw was destitute, and Cowley is said to have helped his friend by introducing him to the Queen. Crashaw died four years later, a priest at the Santa Casa of Loreto in Italy. Johnson's suggestion, presumably, is that only Cowley had the emotional and spiritual generosity to write as follows about Crashaw's death:

> Pardon, my mother Church, if I consent
> That angels led him when from thee he went;
> For ev'n in error sure no danger is
> When joined with so much piety as his.
> Ah, mighty God, with shame I speak'it, and grief,
> Ah, that our greatest faults were in belief!
> And our weak reason were ev'n weaker yet,
> Rather than thus our wills too strong for it.
> His faith, perhaps, in some nice tenents might
> Be wrong; his life, I'm sure, was in the right.
> And I myself a Catholic will be,
> So far, at least, great saint, to pray to thee.

Even here, in a wholly serious poem, Cowley is not entirely solemn. His movement towards the festive and familiar is irresistible: there is, for example, almost a joke on the word 'Catholic'. Here, as elsewhere, Cowley seems able to treat the most significant features of human existence, the most intimate of human bonds, and the most momentous events in human life in a manner which combines lightness and good humour with profound understanding. It seems to have been this combination which appealed to Alexander Pope, who echoed Cowley's lines in his *Essay on Man*: 'For modes of faith let graceless zealots fight; / His can't be wrong, whose life is in the right.' ('The Third Epistle', 305-6). Pope's borrowing indicates that he had discovered in Cowley's lines on Crashaw a commitment to the humane life which transcends even the imperatives of formal religion. The borrowing perhaps suggests why, despite his consciousness of his own contemporaries' reservations, Pope could still judge Cowley to be 'a fine poet, in spite of all his faults', and could affirm his affection for the essential humanity of Cowley's best work:

> Who now reads Cowley? If he pleases yet,
> His moral pleases, not his pointed wit;
> Forgot his epic, nay pindaric art,
> But still I love the language of his heart.

('The First Epistle of the Second Book of Horace Imitated', 75-8)

Notes

1. See John Milton, ed. Thomas Newton, *Paradise Lost* (2 vols., 1749), 1.50; John Dryden, Dedication to *Aureng-Zebe* (1676), in *Works*, ed. Sir Walter Scott and George Saintsbury (15 vols., 1882-93), 5.194; Gilbert Burnet, *Some Passages of the Life and Death of the Right Honourable John, Earl of Rochester* (1680), p. 8; Joseph Spence, *Observations, Anecdotes and Characters of Books and Men*, ed. James M. Osborn (2 vols., Oxford, 1966), 1.189; Alexander Pope, 'The First Epistle of the Second Book of Horace Imitated', ll. 75-8; William Cowper, *The Task*, 4.721-30; Alexander B. Grosart, ed., *The Prose Works of William Wordsworth* (3 vols., 1876), 3.465. For further information on the reception and afterlife of Cowley's work, see Jean Loiseau, *Abraham Cowley's Reputation in England* (Paris, 1931).

2. The standard edition is still that of G. Birkbeck Hill (3 vols., Oxford, 1905).

3. See *Anacreon: with Thomas Stanley's Translation*, ed. A.H. Bullen (1893), p. 221.

4. *Select Works of Mr A. Cowley, In Two Volumes, with a Preface and Notes by [Richard Hurd]* (2 vols., 1772), 2.181.

5. *Boswell's Life of Johnson*, ed. G. Birkbeck Hill, rev. L.F. Powell (6 vols., Oxford, 1950), 5.345.

6. On this poem, see David Hopkins, 'Cowley's Horatian Mice', in *Horace Made New*, ed. Charles Martindale and David Hopkins (Cambridge, 1993), pp. 103-26, 290-3.

7. On this poem, and the *Anacreontics* generally, see Tom Mason, 'Cowley and the Wisdom of Anacreon', *Cambridge Quarterly*, 19 (1990), 103-37.

8. 'On Mr Abraham Cowley His Death and Burial Amongst the Ancient Poets', ll. 29-30.

A Note on Texts

In order to give a clear sense of Cowley's main poetic concerns, this edition groups poems under broad thematic heads, rather than presenting them chronologically. The volume in which each poem was first published is recorded in the Notes. Texts are based on those of the first authorized editions, with mistakes silently corrected, and variants occasionally adopted from other texts (see Notes). Spelling, punctuation, capitals, italics and paragraphing have been modernized, abbreviated titles have been regularized, and the indentation of 'pindaric' (irregular) verse has been normalized, to indicate the number of syllables per line. Quotations in the Introduction have been modernized on similar principles.

The modernizing editor of Cowley is faced with a particular problem, because of the poet's frequent habit of eliding syllables, not only at the beginnings and ends but also in the middle of words (for further discussion, see Introduction). Since our intention in this edition is to assist readers in determining the appropriate scansion, while at the same time printing a text that is immediately intelligible, we have adopted what might be called a 'principled inconsistency' in our treatment of elisions. In instances where elisions are of a familiar kind and the reader is thus unlikely to be puzzled (e.g. 'th' event', 'o'er', 'fathom'st') they are marked with a single inverted comma which indicates, as with the modern apostrophe, that a syllable, usually a vowel, has been omitted in the printed text. But where such a procedure would result in a bafflingly peculiar verbal form (e.g. 'mon'ment', 'tit'lar', 'love't'), we have adopted a convention employed in the seventeenth-century texts, whereby the elision is marked, but all syllables are retained in full in the text.

1. Love and Wine

Anacreontics: or, Some Copies of Verses
Translated Paraphrastically out of Anacreon

1. Love

I'll sing of heroes and of kings,
In mighty numbers, mighty things;
Begin my Muse – but lo, the strings
To my great song rebellious prove;
The strings will sound of nought but Love!
I broke them all, and put on new;
'Tis this, or nothing sure will do.
These sure, said I, will me obey;
These sure heroic notes will play.
Straight I began with thund'ring Jove,
And all th' immortal powers but Love.
Love smiled, and from my' enfeebled lyre
Came gentle airs, such as inspire
Melting love and soft desire.
Farewell, then, heroes, farewell kings,
And mighty numbers, mighty things!
Love tunes my heart just to my strings.

2. Drinking

The thirsty earth soaks up the rain,
And drinks, and gapes for drink again.
The plants suck in the earth, and are
With constant drinking fresh and fair.
The sea itself (which one would think
Should have but little need of drink),

1

Drinks ten thousand rivers up,
So filled that they o'erflow the cup.
The busy sun (and one would guess
By'his drunken fiery face no less)
Drinks up the sea, and when he'has done,
The moon and stars drink up the sun.
They drink and dance by their own light,
They drink and revel all the night.
Nothing in nature's sober found,
But an eternal health goes round.
Fill up the bowl, then, fill it high,
Fill all the glasses there; for why
Should every creature drink but I,
Why, man of morals, tell me why?

10
15
20

3. Beauty

Lib'ral Nature did dispense
To all things arms for their defence;
And some she arms with sin'ewy force,
And some with swiftness in the course;
Some with hard hoofs or forkèd claws,
And some with horns or tuskèd jaws.
And some with scales, and some with wings,
And some with teeth, and some with stings.
Wisdom to man she did afford,
Wisdom for shield, and wit for sword.
What to beauteous womankind,
What arms, what armour has she'assigned?
Beauty is both; for with the fair
What arms, what armour can compare?
What steel, what gold, or diamond,
More impassible is found?
And yet what flame, what lightning, e'er
So great an active force did bear?
They are all weapon, and they dart

2

20   Like porcupines from ev'ry part.
      Who can, alas, their strength express,
      Armed, when they themselves undress,
      Cap-à-pie with nakedness?

4. *The Duel*

      Yes, I will love then, I will love;
      I will not now Love's rebel prove,
      Though I was once his enemy;
      Though ill-advised and stubborn I
5   Did to the combat him defy,
      An helmet, spear, and mighty shield,
      Like some new Ajax, I did wield.
      Love in one hand his bow did take,
      In th' other hand a dart did shake,
10   But yet in vain the dart did throw,
      In vain he often drew the bow.
      So well my armour did resist,
      So oft by flight the blow I missed.
      But, when I thought all danger past,
15   His quiver emptied quite at last;
      Instead of arrow, or of dart,
      He shot himself into my heart.
      The living and the killing arrow
      Ran through the skin, the flesh, the blood,
20   And broke the bones, and scorched the marrow;
      No trench or work of life withstood.
      In vain I now the walls maintain,
      I set out guards and scouts in vain,
      Since th' en'emy does within remain.
25   In vain a breastplate now I wear,
      Since in my breast the foe I bear.
      In vain my feet their swiftness try;
      For from the body can they fly?

5. *Age*

Oft am I by the women told,
Poor Anacre'on, thou grow'st old!
Look how thy hairs are falling all;
Poor Anacre'on, how they fall!
5   Whether I grow old or no,
By th' effects I do not know.
This I know, without be'ing told,
'Tis time to live, if I grow old;
'Tis time short pleasures now to take,
10   Of little life the best to make,
And manage wisely the last stake.

6. *The Account*

When all the stars are by thee told
(The endless sums of heav'nly gold),
Or when the hairs are reckoned all,
From sickly Autumn's head that fall,
5   Or when the drops that make the sea,
Whilst all her sands thy counters be;
Thou, then, and thou alone, mayst prove
Th' aríthmetician of my love.
An hundred loves at Athens score;
10   At Corinth write an hundred more:
Fair Corinth does such beauties bear,
So few is an escaping there.
Write then at Chios seventy-three;
Write then at Lesbos – let me see –
15   Write me at Lesbos ninety down,
Full ninety loves, and half a one.
And, next to these, let me present
The fair Ionian regiment;
And next the Carian company;
20   Five hundred both, effectively.

4

Three hundred more at Rhodes and Crete;
Three hundred 'tis, I'm sure, complete.
For arms at Crete each face does bear,
And ev'ry eye's an archer there.
25 Go on; this stop why dost thou make?
Thou think'st, perhaps, that I mistake.
Seems this to thee too great a sum?
Why many'a thousand are to come;
The mighty Xerxes could not boast
30 Such diff'rent nations in his host.
On, for my love, if thou be'st weary,
Must find some better secretary!
I have not yet my Persian told,
Nor yet my Syrian loves enrolled,
35 Nor Indian, nor Arabian;
Nor Cyprian loves, nor African;
Nor Scythian, nor Italian flames;
There's a whole map behind of names;
Of gentle loves i' th' temp'rate zone,
40 And cold ones in the frigid one;
Cold frozen loves with which I pine,
And parchèd loves beneath the line.

7. *Gold*

A mighty pain to love it is,
And 'tis a pain that pain to miss;
But of all pains the greatest pain
It is to love, but love in vain.
5 Virtue now, nor noble blood,
Nor wit, by love is understood,
Gold alone does passion move,
Gold monopolizes love!
A curse on her, and on the man,
10 Who this traffic first began!
A curse on him who found the ore!

A curse on him who digged the store!
A curse on him who did refine'it!
A curse on him who first did coin'it!
15   A curse all curses else above
On him who used it first in love!
Gold begets in brethren hate;
Gold in families debate;
Gold does friendships separate;
20   Gold does civil wars create;
These the smallest harms of it!
Gold, alas, does love beget.

8. *The Epicure*

Fill the bowl with rosy wine!
Around our temples roses twine!
And let us cheerfully awhile
Like the wine and roses smile.
5   Crowned with roses we contemn
Gyges' wealthy diadem.
Today is ours; what do we fear?
Today is ours; we have it here.
Let's treat it kindly, that it may
10   Wish, at least, with us to stay.
Let's banish business, banish sorrow;
To the gods belongs tomorrow.

9. *Another*

Underneath this myrtle shade,
On flow'ry beds supinely laid,
With od'orous oils my head o'erflowing,
And around it roses growing,
5   What should I do but drink away
The heat and troubles of the day?

In this more-than-kingly state,
Love himself shall on me wait.
Fill to me, Love, nay, fill it up;
And mingled cast into the cup,
Wit, and mirth, and noble fires,
Vig'orous health, and gay desires.
The wheel of life no less will stay
In a smooth than rugged way.
Since it equally does flee,
Let the motion pleasant be.
Why do'we precious ointments show'r,
Nobler wines why do we pour,
Beauteous flowers why do we spread,
Upon the mon'uments of the dead?
Nothing they but dust can show,
Or bones that hasten to be so.
Crown me with roses whilst I live,
Now your wines and ointments give.
After death I nothing crave,
Let me'alive my pleasures have;
All are Stoics in the grave.

10. The Grasshopper

Happy insect, what can be
In happiness compared to thee?
Fed with nourishment divine,
The dewy morning's gentle wine!
Nature waits upon thee still,
And thy verdant cup does fill;
'Tis filled wherever thou dost tread;
Nature self's thy Ganymede.
Thou dost drink, and dance, and sing,
Happier than the happiest king!
All the fields which thou dost see,
All the plants belong to thee,

7

All that summer hours produce,
Fertile made with early juice.
15 Man for thee does sow and plough;
Farmer he, and landlord thou!
Thou dost innocently joy,
Nor does thy luxury destroy;
The shepherd gladly heareth thee,
20 More harmonious than he.
Thee country hinds with gladness hear,
Prophet of the ripened year!
Thee Phoebus loves, and does inspire;
Phoebus is himself thy sire.
25 To thee, of all things upon earth,
Life is no longer than thy mirth.
Happy insect, happy thou,
Dost neither age, nor winter know!
But when thou'st drunk, and danced, and sung
30 Thy fill, the flow'ry leaves among
(Voluptuous, and wise withal,
Epicurean animal!),
Sated with thy summer feast,
Thou retir'st to endless rest.

11. *The Swallow*

Foolish prater, what dost thou
So early at my window do,
With thy tuneless serenade?
Well it'had been had Tereus made
5 Thee as dumb as Philomel;
There his knife had done but well.
In thy undiscovered nest
Thou dost all the winter rest,
And dreamest o'er thy summer joys,
10 Free from the stormy season's noise;
Free from the'ill thou'st done to me;

8

Who disturbs, or seeks out thee?
Hadst thou all the charming notes
Of all the wood's poetic throats,
All thy art could never pay
What thou'st ta'en from me away;
Cruel bird, thou'st ta'en away
A dream out of my arms today,
A dream that ne'er must equalled be
By all that waking eyes may see.
Thou, this damage to repair,
Nothing half so sweet or fair,
Nothing half so good canst bring,
Though men may say thou bring'st the spring.

15

20

Elegy upon Anacreon,
who was Choked by a Grape Stone
Spoken by the God of Love

How shall I lament thine end,
My best servant, and my friend?
Nay, and if from 'a deity
So much deified as I,
It sound not too profane and odd,
O my master, and my god!
For 'tis true, most mighty poet
(Though I like not men should know it),
I'm in naked nature less,
Less by much than in thy dress.
All thy verse is softer far
Than the downy feathers are
Of my wings, or of my arrows,
Of my mother's doves or sparrows;
Sweet as lovers' freshest kisses,
Or their riper foll'owing blisses,

5

10

15

Graceful, cleanly, smooth, and round,
All with Venus' girdle bound;
And thy life was all the while
Kind and gentle as thy style.
The smooth-paced hours of ev'ry day
Glided num'rously away.
Like thy verse each hour did pass,
Sweet and short, like that it was.
    Some do but their youth allow me,
Just what they by nature owe me,
The time that's mine, and not their own,
The certain tribute of my crown;
When they grow old, they grow to be
Too busy, or too wise for me.
Thou wert wiser, and didst know
None too wise for love can grow;
Love was with thy life entwined,
Close as heat with fire is joined;
A powerful brand prescribed the date
Of thine, like Meleager's fate.
Th' *antíperístasis* of age
More inflamed thy am'orous rage,
Thy silver hairs yielded me more
Than even golden curls before.
    Had I the power of creation,
As I have of generation,
Where I the matter must obey,
And cannot work plate out of clay,
My creatures should be all like thee,
'Tis thou shouldst their idea be.
They, like thee, should throughly hate
Business, honour, title, state;
Other wealth they should not know,
But what my living mines bestow;
The pomp of kings, they should confess,
At their crownings to be less
Than a lover's humblest guise,
When at his mistress' feet he lies.

10

Rumour they no more should mind
Than men safe-landed do the wind;
Wisdom itself they should not hear,
When it presumes to be severe;
Beauty alone they should admire,
Nor look at Fortune's vain attire,
Nor ask what parents it can show;
With dead or old it' has nought to do.
They should not love yet all or any,
But very much, and very many;
All their life should gilded be
With mirth, and wit, and gaiety;
Well rememb'ring, and applying
The necessity of dying.
Their cheerful heads should always wear
All that crowns the flow'ry year.
They should always laugh, and sing,
And dance, and strike th' harmonious string.
Verse should from their tongue so flow,
As if it in the mouth did grow,
As swiftly answ'ring their command,
As tunes obey the artful hand.
And whilst I do thus discover
Th' ingredients of a happy lover,
'Tis, my Anacre'on, for thy sake
I of the grape no mention make.

Till my 'Anacre'on by thee fell,
Cursèd plant, I loved thee well;
And 'twas oft my wanton use
To dip my arrows in thy juice.
Cursèd plant, 'tis true, I see,
Th' old report that goes of thee,
That, with giants' blood the earth
Stained and poisoned, gave thee birth,
And now thou wreak'st thy ancient spite
On men in whom the gods delight.
Thy patron, Bacchus, 'tis no wonder,
Was brought forth in flames and thunder;

In rage, in quarrels, and in fights,
Worse than his tigers, he delights;
95 In all our heav'n I think there be
No such ill-natured god as he.
Thou pretendest, trait'rous wine,
To be the Muses' friend and mine.
With love and wit thou dost begin,
100 False fires, alas, to draw us in!
Which, if our course we by them keep,
Misguide to madness or to sleep;
Sleep were well; thou'st learnt a way
To death itself now to betray.
105   It grieves me when I see what fate
Does on the best of mankind wait.
Poets or lovers let them be,
'Tis neither love nor poesy
Can arm, against Death's smallest dart,
110 The poet's head, or lover's heart;
But when their life, in its decline
Touches th' inevitable line,
All the world's mortal to 'em then,
And wine is aconite to men;
115 Nay, in Death's hand the grape stone proves
As strong as thunder is in Jove's.

The Chronicle : A Ballad

1

Margarita first possessed,
  If I remember well, my breast;
  Margarita first of all;
But when awhile the wanton maid
5 With my restless heart had played,
  Martha took the flying ball.

2

Martha soon did it resign
    To the beauteous Catharine.
    Beauteous Catharine gave place
(Though loth and angry she to part
With the possession of my heart)
    To Eliza's conqu'ring face.

3

Eliza till this hour might reign,
    Had she not evil counsels ta'en.
    Fundamental laws she broke,
And still new favourites she chose,
Till up in arms my passions rose,
    And cast away her yoke.

4

Mary then and gentle Anne
    Both to reign at once began.
    Alternately they swayed,
And sometimes Mary was the fair,
And sometimes Anne the crown did wear,
    And sometimes both I'obeyed.

5

Another Mary then arose,
    And did rig'orous laws impose;
    A mighty tyrant she!
Long, alas, should I have been
Under that iron-sceptered queen,
    Had not Rebecca set me free.

6

When fair Rebecca set me free,
    'Twas then a golden time with me;
    But soon those pleasures fled,
For the gracious princess died
In her youth and beauty's pride,
    And Judith reignèd in her stead.

7

One month, three days, and half an hour
    Judith held the sov'reign power;
    Wondrous, beautiful her face,
But so weak and small her wit,
That she to govern was unfit,
    And so Susanna took her place.

8

But when Isabella came,
    Armed with a resistless flame,
    And th' artillery of her eye,
Whilst she proudly marched about,
Greater conquests to find out,
    She beat out Susan by the by.

9

But in her place I then obeyed
    Black-eyed Bess, her viceroy-maid,
    To whom ensued a vacancy.
Thousand worse passions then possessed
The interregnum of my breast;
    Bless me from such an anarchy!

10

Gentle Henrietta then
    And a third Mary next began,
    Then Joan, and Jane, and Audria,
And then a pretty Thomasine,
And then another Katharine,
    And then a long *et cetera*.

11

But should I now to you relate
    The strength and riches of their state,
    The powder, patches, and the pins,
The ribbons, jewels, and the rings,
The lace, the paint, and warlike things,
    That make up all their magazines;

12

If I should tell the pol'itic arts
    To take and keep men's hearts,
    The letters, embassies, and spies,
The frowns, and smiles, and flatteries,
The quarrels, tears, and perjuries,
    Numberless, nameless mysteries!

13

And all the little lime-twigs laid
    By Matchavil the waiting-maid,
    I more voluminous should grow
(Chiefly if I like them should tell
All change of weathers that befell)
    Than Holinshed or Stow.

But I will briefer with them be,
    Since few of them were long with me.
An higher and a nobler strain
My present emperess does claim,
Heleonora, first o' th' name,
    Whom God grant long to reign!

80

Ode : Acme and Septimius, out of Catullus

Whilst on Septimius' panting breast
(Meaning nothing less than rest)
Acme leaned her loving head,
Thus the pleased Septimius said:

'My dearest Acme, if I be
Once alive, and love not thee
With a passion far above
All that e'er was callèd love,
In a Lybian desert may
I become some lion's prey;
Let him, Acme, let him tear
My breast when Acme is not there.'

The god of love who stood to hear him
(The god of love was always near him),
Pleased and tickled with the sound,
Sneezed aloud, and, all around,
The little Loves that waited by
Bowed, and blessed the augury.

Acme', enflamed with what he said,
Reared her gently-bending head;
And, her purple mouth with joy

5

10

15

20

Stretching to the'delicious boy,
Twice (and twice could scarce suffice)
She kissed his drunken, rolling eyes.

25 'My little life, my all,' said she,
'So may we ever servants be
To this best god, and ne'er retain
Our hated liberty again!
So may thy passion last for me,
30 As I a passion have for thee,
Greater and fiercer much than can
Be conceived by thee, a man!
Into my marrow is it gone,
Fixed and settled in the bone;
35 It reigns not only in my heart,
But runs, like life, through every part.'

She spoke; the god of love aloud
Sneezed again, and all the crowd
Of little Loves that waited by
40 Bowed, and blessed the augury.

This good omen thus from heav'n
Like a happy signal giv'n,
Their loves and lives (all four) embrace,
And hand in hand run all the race.
45 To poor Septimius (who did now
Nothing else but Acme grow)
Acme's bosom was alone
The whole world's imperial throne;
And to faithful Acme's mind
50 Septimius was all humankind.

If the gods would please to be
But advised for once by me,
I'd advise 'em, when they spy
Any'illustrious piety,
55 To reward her, if'it be she,

To reward him, if it be he,
With such a husband, such a wife,
With Acme's and Septimius' life.

Ode: In Imitation of Horace his Ode [Book 1, Ode 5]

1

To whom now, Pyrrha, art thou kind?
    To what heart-ravished lover
Dost thou thy golden locks unbind,
    Thy hidden sweets discover;
5   And with large bounty open set
All the bright stores of thy rich cabinet?

2

Ah, simple youth! how oft will he
    Of thy changed faith complain,
And his own fortunes find to be
10   So airy and so vain,
    Of so chameleon-like an hue,
That still their colour changes with it too!

3

How oft, alas, will he admire
    The blackness of the skies,
15   Trembling to hear the winds sound higher,
    And see the billows rise!
    Poor unexperienced he,
Who ne'er, alas, before had been at sea!

4

He'enjoys thy calmy sunshine now,
 And no breath stirring hears;
In the clear heaven of thy brow
 No smallest cloud appears.
He sees thee gentle, fair, and gay,
And trusts the faithless April of thy May.

5

Unhappy, thrice unhappy, he
 To whom thou' untried dost shine!
But there's no danger now for me,
 Since o'er Loreto's shrine,
In witness of the shipwreck past,
My consecrated vessel hangs at last.

2. Friends and Heroes

Brutus

1

Excellent Brutus, of all human race
The best, till nature was improved by grace;
Till men above themselves Faith raisèd more
 Than Reason above beasts before.
5 Virtue was thy life's centre, and from thence
Did silently and constantly dispense
 The gentle, vig'orous influence
To all the wide and fair circumference;
And all the parts upon it leaned so easily,
10 Obeyed the mighty force so willingly,
That none could discord or disorder see
 In all their contrariety;
Each had his motion natural and free,
And the whole no more moved than the whole world
          could be.

2

15 From thy strict rule some think that thou didst swerve
(Mistaken, honest men!) in Caesar's blood;
What mercy could the tyrant's life deserve
From him who killed himself, rather than serve?
Th' heroic exaltatíons of good
20 Are so far from understood,
We count it vice; alas, our sight's so ill,
That things which swiftest move seem to stand still;
We look not upon Virtue in her height,
On her supreme idea, brave and bright,
25 In the orig'inal light;
 But as her beams reflected pass

Through our own nature, or ill custom's glass;
    And 'tis no wonder, so,
     If with dejected eye
30   In standing pools we seek the sky,
That stars, so high above, should seem to us below.

3

    Can we stand by and see
Our mother robbed, and bound, and ravished be,
    Yet not to her assistance stir,
35   Pleased with the strength and beauty of the ravisher?
    Or shall we fear to kill him, if before
     The cancelled name of friend he bore?
     Ingrateful Brutus do they call?
Ingrateful Caesar, who could Rome enthral!
40 An act more barb'arous and unnatural
    (In th' exact balance of true virtue tried)
    Than his successor Nero's parricide!
     There's none but Brutus could deserve
    That all men else should wish to serve,
45   And Caesar's úsurped place to him should proffer;
None can deserve'it but he who would refuse the offer.

4

Ill Fate assumed a body thee to'affright,
And wrapped itself i' th' terrors of the night;
'I'll meet thee at Philippi,' said the sprite;
50   'I'll meet thee there,' saidst thou,
    With such a voice, and such a brow,
As put the trembling ghost to sudden flight;
    It vanished, as a taper's light
    Goes out when spir'its appear in sight.
55 One would have thought'it had heard the morning
                       crow,
    Or seen her well-appointed star

21

Come marching up the eastern hill afar.
　　Nor durst it in Philippi's field appear,
　　　　But unseen attacked thee there;
60　　Had it presumed in any shape thee to oppose,
　　　Thou wouldst have forced it back upon thy foes;
　　　　Or slain'it, like Caesar, though it be
A conqu'ror and a monarch mightier far than he.

5

　　What joy can human things to us afford,
65　　When we see perish thus, by odd events,
　　　Ill men, and wretched accidents,
The best cause and best man that ever drew a sword?
　　　　　When we see
　　The false Octavius and wild Antony,
70　　　　Godlike Brutus, conquer thee?
　　What can we say, but thine own tragic word:
　　That Virtue, which had worshipped been by thee
As the most solid good, and greatest deity,
　　　By this fatal proof became
75　　　An idol only, and a name?
　　　Hold, noble Brutus, and restrain
　　The bold voice of thy generous disdain;
　　　　These mighty gulfs are yet
　　Too deep for all thy judgement and thy wit.
80　　The time's set forth already which shall quell
　　Stiff Reason, when it offers to rebel;
　　　Which these great secrets shall unseal,
　　　And new philosophies reveal;
　　A few years more, so soon hadst thou not died,
85　　Would have confounded human Virtue's pride,
　　　And showed thee a God crucified.

To Mr Hobbes

1

Vast bodies of philosophy
  I oft have seen and read;
  But all are bodies dead,
  Or bodies by art fashionèd;
I never yet the living soul could see,
    But in thy books and thee.
    'Tis only God can know
Whether the fair idea thou dost show
Agree entirely with His own or no.
    This I dare boldly tell,
'Tis so like truth, 'twill serve our turn as well.
Just, as in nature, thy proportions be,
As full of concord their variety,
As firm the parts upon their centre rest,
And all so solid are, that they, at least
As much as nature, emptiness detest.

2

Long did the mighty Stagirite retain
The universal intellectual reign,
Saw his own country's short-lived leopard slain;
  The stronger Roman eagle did out-fly,
Oft'ner renewed his age, and saw that die.
Mecca itself, in spite of Máhomet, possessed,
  And, chased by a wild deluge from the east,
  His monarchy new planted in the west.
But as in time each great imperial race
Degenerates and gives some new one place;
    So did this noble empire waste,
    Sunk by degrees from glories past,
And in the schoolmen's hands it perished quite at last;
    Then nought but words it grew,
    And those all barb'arous too;

It perished, and it vanished there,
The life and soul breathed out, became but empty air.

3

The fields, which answered well the ancients' plough,
35   Spent and outworn, return no harvest now;
In barren age wild and unglorious lie,
   And boast of past fertility,
The poor relief of present poverty.
    Food and fruit we now must want,
40   Unless new lands we plant.
We break up tombs with sacrilegious hands;
   Old rubbish we remove;
To walk in ruins like vain ghosts we love,
   And with fond divining wands
45   We search among the dead
    For treasures burièd;
Whilst still the lib'ral earth does hold
So many virgin mines of undiscovered gold.

4

The Baltic, Euxine, and the Caspian,
50   And slender-limbed Mediterranean,
Seem narrow creeks to thee, and only fit
For the poor wretched fisher-boats of wit;
Thy nobler vessel the vast ocean tries,
   And nothing sees but seas and skies,
55   Till unknown regions it descries,
Thou great Columbus of the golden lands of new
                    philosophies!
   Thy task was harder much than his;
   For thy learn'd America is
   Not only found out first by thee,
60   And rudely left to future industry;
   But thy eloquence, and thy wit
Has planted, peopled, built, and civ'ilized it.

5

I little thought before
(Nor, being my own self so poor,

65   Could comprehend so vast a store)
That all the wardrobe of rich eloquence
Could have afforded half enough
Of bright, of new, and lasting stuff,
To clothe the mighty limbs of thy gigantic sense.

70   Thy solid reason, like the shield from heav'n
To the Trojan hero giv'n,
Too strong to take a mark from any mortal dart,
Yet shines with gold and gems in ev'ry part,
And wonders on it graved by the learn'd hand of art!

75   A shield that gives delight
Ev'n to the en'emies' sight,
Then, when they're sure to lose the combat by'it.

6

Nor can the snow, which now cold age does shed
Upon thy rev'rend head,

80   Quench or allay the noble fires within;
But all which thou hast been,
And all that youth can be, thou'rt yet!
So fully still dost thou
Enjoy the manhood and the bloom of wit,

85   And all the nat'ural heat, but not the fever too!
So contraries on Etna's top conspire;
Here hoary frosts, and by them breaks out fire!
A sécure peace the faithful neighbours keep;
Th' emboldened snow next to the flame does sleep

90   And, if we weigh, like thee,
Nature and causes, we shall see
That thus it needs must be;
To things immortal, time can do no wrong,
And that which never is to die, for ever must be young.

On the Death of Mr William Hervey

Immodicis brevis est aetas, et rara senectus
Martial

1

It was a dismal and a fearful night,
Scarce could the morn drive on th' unwilling light,
When sleep, death's image, left my troubled breast,
    By something liker death possessed,
My eyes with tears did uncommanded flow,
    And on my soul hung the dull weight
    Of some intolerable fate.
What bell was that? Ah me! too much I know.

2

My sweet companion, and my gentle peer,
Why hast thou left me thus unkindly here,
Thy end for ever, and my life, to moan?
    O, thou hast left me all alone!
Thy soul and body, when death's agony
    Besieged around thy noble heart,
    Did not with more reluctance part,
Than I, my dearest friend, do part from thee.

3

My dearest friend, would I had died for thee!
Life and this world henceforth will tedious be.
Nor shall I know hereafter what to do,
    If once my griefs prove tedious too.
Silent and sad I walk about all day,
    As sullen ghosts stalk speechless by
    Where their hid treasures lie;
Alas, my treasure's gone! Why do I stay?

4

25   He was my friend, the truest friend on earth;
     A strong and mighty influ'ence joined our birth;
     Nor did we envy the most sounding name
         By friendship giv'n of old to fame.
     None but his brethren he and sisters knew,
30   Whom the kind youth preferred to me;
         And ev'n in that we did agree,
     For much above myself I loved them too.

5

     Say, for you saw us, ye immortal lights,
     How oft unwearied have we spent the nights,
35   Till the Ledaean stars, so famed for love,
         Wondered at us from above!
     We spent them not in toys, in lusts, or wine;
         But search of deep philosophy,
         Wit, eloquence, and poetry;
40   Arts which I loved, for they, my friend, were thine.

6

     Ye fields of Cambridge, our dear Cambridge, say,
     Have ye not seen us walking every day?
     Was there a tree about which did not know
         The love betwixt us two?
45   Henceforth, ye gentle trees, for ever fade;
         Or your sad branches thicker join,
         And into darksome shades combine,
     Dark as the grave wherein my friend is laid!

7

     Henceforth, no learnèd youths beneath you sing,
50   Till all the tuneful birds to'your boughs they bring;
     No tuneful birds play with their wonted cheer,
         And call the learnèd youths to hear;

No whistling winds through the glad branches fly;
    But all, with sad solemnity,
55   Mute and unmovèd be,
Mute as the grave wherein my friend does lie.

8

To him my Muse made haste with ev'ry strain,
Whilst it was new and warm yet from the brain;
He loved my worthless rhymes, and, like a friend,
60   Would find out something to commend.
Hence now, my Muse, thou canst not me delight;
    Be this my latest verse,
    With which I now adorn his hearse;
And this my grief, without thy help, shall write.

9

65 Had I a wreath of bays about my brow,
I should contemn that flour'ishing honour now;
Condemn it to the fire, and joy to hear
    It rage and crackle there.
Instead of bays, crown with sad cypress me;
70   Cypress, which tombs does beautify;
    Not Phoebus grieved so much as I
For him who first was made that mournful tree.

10

Large was his soul; as large a soul as e'er
Submitted to inform a body here;
75 High as the place 'twas shortly'in heav'n to have,
    But low and humble as his grave;
So high, that all the Virtues there did come,
    As to their chiefest seat
    Conspicuous and great;
80 So low, that for me too it made a room.

11

He scorned this busy world below, and all
That we, mistaken mortals, pleasure call;
Was filled with inn'ocent gallantry and truth,
    Triumphant o'er the sins of youth.
85   He, like the stars to which he now is gone,
      That shine with beams like flame,
      Yet burn not with the same,
Had all the light of youth, of the fire none.

12

Knowledge he only sought, and so soon caught,
90   As if for him Knowledge had rather sought;
Nor did more learning ever crowded lie
    In such a short mortality.
Whene'er the skilful youth discoursed or writ,
    Still did the notions throng
95   About his el'oquent tongue,
Nor could his ink flow faster than his wit.

13

So strong a wit did Nature to him frame,
As all things but his judgement overcame;
His judgement like the heav'nly moon did show,
100   Temp'ring that mighty sea below.
O, had he lived in learning's world, what bound
    Would have been able to control
    His overpow'ring soul?
We'have lost in him arts that not yet are found.

14

105   His mirth was the pure spir'its of various wit,
Yet never did his God or friends forget;
And when deep talk and wisdom came in view,
    Retired and gave to them their due;

For the rich help of books he always took,
110   Though his own searching mind before
      Was so with notions written o'er,
As if wise Nature had made that her book.

15

So many virtues joined in him, as we
Can scarce pick here and there in history;
115   More than old writers' practice e'er could reach;
      As much as they could ever teach.
These did Religion, Queen of Virtues, sway;
      And all their sacred motions steer,
      Just like the first and highest sphere,
120   Which wheels about, and turns all heav'n one way.

16

With as much zeal, devotion, piety,
He always lived, as other saints do die.
Still with his soul severe account he kept,
      Weeping all debts out ere he slept;
125   Then down in peace and innocence he lay,
      Like the sun's laborious light,
      Which still in water sets at night,
Unsullied with his journey of the day.

17

Wondrous young man, why wert thou made so good,
130   To be snatched hence ere better understood?
Snatched before half of thee enough was seen;
      Thou ripe, and yet thy life but green!
Nor could thy friends take their last, sad farewell;
      But danger and infectious death
135   Maliciously seized on that breath
Where life, spir'it, pleasure always used to dwell.

18

But happy thou, ta'en from this frantic age,
Where Ign'orance and Hypocrisy does rage.
A fitter time for heav'n no soul ere chose,
140   The place now only free from those.
There 'mong the blest thou dost for ever shine,
    And wheresoe'er thou cast'st thy view,
    Upon that white and radiant crew,
See'st not a soul clothed with more light than thine.

19

145   And, if the glorious saints cease not to know
Their wretchèd friends who fight with life below,
Thy flame to me does still the same abide,
    Only more pure and rarefied.
There, whilst immortal hymns thou dost rehearse,
150   Thou dost with holy pity see
    Our dull and earthly poesy,
Where grief and mis'ery can be joined with verse.

On the Death of Mr Crashaw

Poet and saint: to thee alone are giv'n
The two most sacred names of earth and heav'n;
The hard and rarest union which can be
Next that of Godhead with humanity!
5   Long did the Muses banished slaves abide,
And built vain pyramids to mortal pride;
Like Moses, thou (though spells and charms withstand)
Hast brought them nobly home, back to their Holy Land.
    Ah, wretched we – poets of earth! but thou
10   Wert, living, the same poet which thou'rt now.
Whilst angels sing to thee their airs divine,
And joy in an applause so great as thine.

Equal society with them to hold,
Thou needst not make new songs, but say the old.
15 And they, kind spir'its, shall all rejoice to see
How little less than they, exalted man may be.
Still the old heathen gods in numbers dwell,
The heav'nliest thing on earth still keeps up hell.
Nor have we yet quite purged the Christian land;
20 Still idols here, like calves at Bethel, stand.
And though Pan's death long since all or'acles breaks,
Yet still in rhyme the fiend Apollo speaks;
Nay, with the worst of heathen dotage we,
Vain men, the monster Woman deify;
25 Find stars, and tie our fates there in a face,
And Paradise in them by whom we lost it, place.
What diff'rent faults corrupt our Muses thus?
Wanton as girls, as old wives fabulous!
    Thy spotless Muse, like Mary, did contain
30 The boundless Godhead; she did well disdain
That her eternal verse employed should be
On a less subject than eternity;
And for a sacred mistress scorned to take
But her, whom God himself scorned not his spouse to make.
35 It, in a kind, her miracle did do;
A fruitful mother was, and virgin too.
    How well, blest swan, did Fate contrive thy death,
And made thee render up thy tuneful breath
In thy great mistress' arms! thou most divine
40 And richest off'ring of Loreto's shine!
Where like some holy sacrifice to'expire,
A fever burns thee, and Love lights the fire.
Angels, they say, brought the famed chapel there,
And bore the sacred load in triumph through the air.
45 'Tis surer much they brought thee there, and they,
And thou, their charge, went singing all the way.
 Pardon, my mother Church, if I consent
That angels led him when from thee he went;
For ev'n in error sure no danger is
50 When joined with so much piety as his.

Ah, mighty God, with shame I speak'it, and grief,
Ah, that our greatest faults were in belief!
And our weak reason were ev'n weaker yet,
Rather than thus our wills too strong for it.
His faith, perhaps, in some nice tenents might
Be wrong; his life, I'm sure, was in the right.
And I myself a Catholic will be,
So far, at least, great saint, to pray to thee.
     Hail, bard triumphant, and some care bestow
On us, the poets militant below!
Opposed by our old en'emy, adverse Chance,
Attacked by Envy, and by Ignorance,
Enchained by Beauty, tortured by Desires,
Exposed by Tyrant-Love to savage beasts and fires.
Thou from low earth in nobler flames didst rise,
And, like Elijah, mount alive the skies.
Elisha-like (but with a wish much less,
More fit thy greatness, and my littleness)
Lo, here I beg – I whom thou once didst prove
So humble to esteem, so good to love –
Not that thy spir'it might on me doubled be
I ask, but half thy mighty spir'it for me.
And when my Muse soars with so strong a wing,
'Twill learn of things divine, and first of thee, to sing.

Ode upon Dr Harvey

1

Coy Nature (which remained, though agèd grown,
A beauteous virgin still, enjoyed by none,
     Nor seen unveiled by anyone),
When Harvey's violent passion she did see,
     Began to tremble and to flee;
Took sanctu'ary, like Daphne, in a tree;
There Daphne's lover stopped, and thought it much

33

The very leaves of her to touch;
But Harvey, our Apollo, stopped not so;
10   Into the bark and root he after her did go!
   No smallest fibres of a plant,
For which the eye-beam's point doth sharpness want,
   His passage after her withstood.
What should she do? Through all the moving wood
15   Of lives endowed with sense she took her flight;
Harvey pursues, and keeps her still in sight.
But as the deer, long-hunted, takes a flood,
She leaped at last into the winding streams of blood;
Of man's Meander all the purple reaches made,
20   Till at the heart she stayed;
   Where, turning head, and at a bay,
Thus by well-purgèd ears was she o'erheard to say:

2

   'Here, sure, I shall be safe,' said she,
   'None will be able sure to see
25   This my retreat, but only He
     Who made both it and me.
The heart of man what art can e'er reveal?
   A wall impervious between
   Divides the very parts within,
30   And doth the heart of man ev'n from itself conceal.'
   She spoke; but, ere she was aware,
     Harvey was with her there;
And held this slipp'ry Proteus in a chain,
Till all her mighty myst'eries she descried;
35   Which from his wit th' attempt before to hide
Was the first thing that Nature did in vain.

3

He the young practice of new life did see,
Whilst, to conceal its toilsome poverty,
It for a living wrought, both hard and privately.
40   Before the liver understood

        The noble scarlet dye of blood;
        Before one drop was by it made,
        Or brought into it, to set up the trade;
        Before the untaught heart began to beat
45   The tuneful march to vital heat;
        From all the souls that living buildings rear,
        Whether employed for earth, or sea, or air;
        Whether it in the womb or egg be wrought;
        A strict account to him is hourly brought
50   How the great fabric does proceed,
        What time, and what materials, it does need;
        He so exactly does the work survey,
        As if he hired the workers by the day.

                            4
        Thus Harvey sought for Truth in Truth's own book,
55   The creatures, which by God himself was writ;
            And wisely thought 'twas fit,
        Not to read comments only úpon it,
        But on th' original itself to look.
        Methinks in art's great circle others stand
60   Locked up together hand in hand;
            Everyone leads as he is led;
            The same bare path they tread,
        And dance like fairies a fantastic round,
        But neither change their motion nor their ground;
65   Had Harvey to this road confined his wit,
        His noble circle of the blood had been untrodden yet.
            Great Doctor, th' art of curing's cured by thee!
            We now thy patient, Physic, see
            From all inveterate diseases free,
70   Purged of old errors by thy care,
            New-dieted, put forth to clearer air;
            It now will strong and healthful prove;
        Itself before lethargic lay, and could not move!

These useful secrets to his pen we owe,
75   And thousands more 'twas ready to bestow;
Of which a barb'arous war's unlearnèd rage
    Has robbed the ruined age;
O cruel loss! as if the golden fleece,
  With so much cost and labour bought,
80   And from afar by a great hero brought,
  Had sunk ev'n in the ports of Greece.
O cursèd war! who can forgive thee this?
  Houses and towns may rise again,
    And ten times easier'it is
85   To rebuild Paul's than any work of his;
That mighty task none but himself can do,
    Nay, scarce himself too, now;
For though his wit the force of age withstand,
His body', alas, and time it must command;
90   And Nature now, so long by him surpassed,
Will sure have her revenge on him at last.

3. How to Live

The Tree of Knowledge:
That there is no Knowledge
(Against the Dogmatists)

1

The sacred tree 'midst the fair orchard grew;
    The phoenix Truth did on it rest,
    And built his perfumed nest;
That right Porphyrian tree which did true logic show.
5   Each leaf did learnèd notions give,
    And th' apples were demonstrative;
    So clear their colour and divine,
The very shade they cast did other lights outshine.

2

'Taste not,' said God, ''tis mine and angels' meat;
10   A certain death doth sit
    Like an ill worm i' th' core of it.
Ye cannot know and live, nor live or know and eat.'
    Thus spoke God, yet man did go
    Ignorantly on to know;
15   Grew so more blind, and she
Who tempted him to this, grew yet more blind than he.

3

The only science man by this did get
    Was but to know he nothing knew;
    He straight his nakedness did view,
20 His ign'orant poor estate, and was ashamed of it.

Yet searches probabilities,
And rhetoric, and fallacies,
And seeks by useless pride,
With slight and with'ring leaves that nakedness to hide.

4

25   'Henceforth,' said God, 'the wretched sons of earth
Shall sweat for food in vain,
That will not long sustain;
And bring with labour forth each fond abortive birth.
That serpent, too, their pride,
30   Which aims at things denied;
That learn'd and el'oquent lust;
Instead of mounting high, shall creep upon the dust.'

Life

Nascentes morimur (Manilius)

1

We're ill by these grammarians used;
We are abused by words, grossly abused;
From the maternal tomb,
To the grave's fruitful womb.
5   We call here 'life'; but 'life''s a name
That nothing here can truly claim;
This wretched inn, where we scarce stay to bait,
We call our dwelling-place;
We call one step a race;
10   But angels, in their full enlightened state,
Angels who live, and know what 'tis to be,
Who all the nonsense of our language see;
Who speak things, and our words, their ill-drawn
pictures, scorn;

When we, by'a foolish figure, say,
  'Behold an old man dead!' then they
Speak properly, and cry, 'Behold a man-child born!'

2

My eyes are opened, and I see
Through the transparent fallacy;
Because we seem wisely to talk
Like men of business; and for business walk
  From place to place,
And mighty voyages we take,
And mighty journeys seem to make,
O'er sea and land, the little point that has no space;
 Because we fight, and battles gain;
 Some 'captives' call, and say, 'the rest are slain';
Because we heap up yellow earth, and so
Rich, valiant, wise, and virt'uous seem to grow;
Because we draw a long nobility
From hieroglyphic proofs of heraldry,
And impudently talk of a 'posterity',
 And like Egyptian chroniclers,
 Who write of twenty thousand years,
 With maravedies make th' account,
That single time might to a sum amount;
We grow at last by custom to believe
 That réally we live;
Whilst all these shadows that for things we take
Are but the empty dreams which in death's sleep we
         make.

3

But these fantastic errors of our dream
 Lead us to solid wrong;
We pray to God our friends' torments to pr'olong,
 And wish unchar'itably for them
To be as long a-dying as Methusalem.

39

45   The ripened soul longs from his pris'on to come;
       But we would seal and sow up, if we could, the womb;
         We seek to close and plaster up by art
           The cracks and breaches of th' extended shell,
               And in that narrow cell
50   Would rudely force to dwell
       The noble vig'orous bird already winged to part.

Against Hope

1

       Hope, whose weak being ruined is
       Alike, if it succeed and if it miss;
       Whom good or ill does equally confound,
       And both the horns of Fate's dilemma wound;
5   Vain shadow, which dost vanish quite,
             Both at full noon and perfect night!
       The stars have not a possibility
               Of blessing thee;
       If things then from their end we happy call,
10   'Tis Hope is the most hopeless thing of all!

2

       Hope, thou bold taster of delight,
       Who, whilst thou shouldst but taste, devour'st it quite!
       Thou bring'st us an estate, yet leav'st us poor,
       By clogging it with legacies before!
15   The joys which we entire should wed,
             Come déflowered virgins to our bed;
       Good fortunes without gain imported be,
             Such mighty custom's paid to thee.
       For joy, like wine, kept close does better taste;
20   If it take air before, its spirits waste.

3

Hope, Fortune's cheating lottery!
Where for one prize an hundred blanks there be;
Fond archer, Hope, who tak'st thy aim so far,
That still or short or wide thine arrows are!
25   Thin, empty cloud, which th' eye deceives
    With shapes that our own fancy gives!
A cloud, which gilt and painted now appears,
    But must drop presently in tears!
When thy false beams o'er Reason's light prevail,
30 By *ignes fatui* for north stars we sail.

4

Brother of Fear, more gaily clad!
The merrier fool o' th' two, yet quite as mad;
Sire of Repentance, child of fond Desire!
That blow'st the chemics' and the lovers' fire,
35   Leading them still insens'ibly on
    By the strange witchcraft of 'Anon!'
By thee the one does changing Nature, through
    Her endless labyrinths, pursue;
And th' other chases Woman, whilst she goes
40 More ways and turns than hunted Nature knows.

For Hope

1

Hope, of all ills that men endure
The only cheap and universal cure!
Thou captive's freedom, and thou sick man's health!
Thou loser's vict'ory, and thou beggar's wealth!
5   Thou manna, which from heav'n we eat,
    To every taste a sev'ral meat!

Thou strong retreat, thou sure-entailed estate,
  Which nought has power to alienate.
Thou pleasant, honest flatt'rer; for none
10   Flatter unhappy men, but thou alone!

2

  Hope, thou first-fruits of happiness;
Thou gentle dawning of a bright success;
Thou good prepar'ative, without which our joy
Does work too strong, and, whilst it cures, destroy;
15   Who out of Fortune's reach dost stand,
    And art a blessing still in hand.
Whilst thee, her earnest-money, we retain,
  We certain are to gain,
Whether she'her bargain break, or else fulfil;
20 Thou only good, not worse for ending ill!

3

  Brother of Faith, 'twixt whom and thee
The joys of heav'n and earth divided be.
Though Faith be heir, and have the fixed estate,
Thy portion yet in moveables is great.
25   Happiness itself's all one
    In thee, or in possessíon!
Only the future's thine, the present his;
  Thine's the more hard and noble bliss;
Best apprehender of our joys; which hast
30 So long a reach, and yet canst hold so fast!

4

  Hope, thou sad lovers' only friend;
Thou way, that mayst dispute it with the end!
For love I fear 's a fruit that does delight
The taste itself less than the smell and sight.
35   Fruition more deceitful is

42

Than thou canst be when thou dost miss;
Men leave thee by obtaining, and straight flee
Some other way again to thee;
And that's a pleasant country, without doubt,
40   To which all soon return that travel out.

To the New Year

1

Great Janus (who dost, sure, my mistress view
With all thine eyes, yet think'st them all too few),
If thy fore-face do see
No better things prepared for me,
5   Than did thy face behind;
If still her breast must shut against me be
(For 'tis not Peace that temple's gate does bind);
O let my life, if thou so many deaths a-coming find,
With thine old year its voyage take,
10   Borne down that stream of time which no return can
make!

2

Alas, what need I thus to pray?
Th' old avaricious year,
Whether I would or no, will bear
At least a part of me away;
15   His well-horsed troops, the months, and days, and
hours,
Though never anywhere they stay,
Make in their passage all their prey;
The months, days, hours that march i' th' rear can find
Nought of value left behind.
20   All the good wine of life our drunken youth devours;

43

Sourness and lees, which to the bottom sink,
    Remain for latter years to drink;
  Until, someone offended with the taste,
The vessel breaks, and out the wretched relics run at last.

3

25   If then, young year, thou needs must come,
      (For in Time's fruitful womb
   The birth beyond his time can never tarry,
      Nor ever can miscarry),
  Choose thy attendants well; for 'tis not thee
30   We fear, but 'tis thy company;
Let neither Loss of Friends, or Fame, or Liberty,
  Nor pining Sickness, nor tormenting Pain,
  Nor Sadness, nor uncleanly Poverty,
    Be seen among thy train;
35   Nor let thy liv'ery be
Either black sin, or gaudy vanity;
  Nay, if thou lov'st me, gentle year,
  Let not so much as Love be there;
Vain, fruitless Love, I mean; for, gentle year,
40   Although I fear,
  There's of this caution little need,
   Yet, gentle year, take heed
    How thou dost make
    Such a mistake;
45   Such Love I mean, alone,
As by thy cruel predecessors has been shown;
  For though I'have too much cause to doubt it,
I fain would try for once if life can live without it.

4

Into the future times why do we pry,
50   And seek to antedate our misery?
Like jealous men why are we longing still
To see the thing which only seeing makes an ill?

'Tis well the face is veiled; for 'twere a sight
    That would ev'n happiest men affright;
55   And something still they'd spy that would destroy
      The past and present joy.
    In whatsoever character
      The Book of Fate is writ,
    'Tis well we understand not it;
60   We should grow mad with little learning there;
Upon the brink of ev'ry ill we did foresee,
    Undecently and foolishly
We should stand shiv'ring, and but slowly venture
    The fatal flood to enter;
65   Since, willing or unwilling, we must do'it,
They feel least cold and pain who plunge at once into'it.

Seneca, from *Thyestes*: Act 2, Chorus

Upon the slipp'ry tops of human state,
    The gilded pinnacles of fate,
Let others proudly stand, and for a while,
    The giddy danger to beguile,
5   With joy and with disdain look down on all,
    Till their heads turn, and down they fall.
Me, O ye gods, on earth, or else so near
    That I no fall to earth may fear,
And, O ye gods, at a good distance seat
10   From the long ruins of the great!
Here wrapped in th' arms of Quiet let me lie;
Quiet, companion of Obscurity.
Here let my life with as much silence slide
    As time that measures it does glide;
15   Nor let the breath of Infamy or Fame
From town to town echo about my name;
Nor let my homely death embroidered be
    With 'scutcheon or with elegy.

An old plebeian let me die;
20 Alas, all then are such, as well as I;
  To him, alas, to him, I fear,
The face of Death will terrible appear,
Who, in his life, flatt'ring his senseless pride
By being known to all the world beside,
25 Does not himself, when he is dying, know,
Nor what he is, nor whither he's to go.

Horace: Book 3, Ode 1

1

Hence, ye profane; I hate ye all;
 Both the great vulgar, and the small.
To virgin minds, which yet their native whiteness hold,
 Not yet discoloured with the love of gold
5   (That jaundice of the soul,
 Which makes it look so gilded and so foul),
 To you, ye very few, these truths I tell;
The Muse inspires my song; hark, and observe it well.

2

We look on men, and wonder at such odds
10 'Twixt things that were the same by birth;
 We look on kings as giants of the earth;
These giants are but pigmies to the gods.
  The humblest bush and proudest oak
Are but of equal proof against the thunder-stoke.
15 Beauty, and strength, and wit, and wealth, and power
  Have their short flour'ishing hour,
 And love to see themselves and smile,
 And joy in their pre-eminence awhile;
  Ev'n so in the same land,
20 Poor weeds, rich corn, gay flowers together stand;
Alas, Death mows down all with an impartial hand.

3

And all you men, whom greatness does so please,
  Ye feast, I fear, like Damocles;
    If you your eyes could upwards move
25   (But you, I fear, think nothing is above),
You would perceive by what a little thread
  The sword still hangs over your head.
    No tide of wine would drown your cares;
    No mirth or music over-noise your fears.
30 The fear of death would you so watchful keep,
As not to'admit the image of it, sleep.

4

Sleep is a god too proud to wait in palaces,
  And yet so humble too, as not to scorn
    The meanest country cottages;
35   His poppy grows among the corn.
The halcyon sleep will never build his nest
  In any stormy breast.
    'Tis not enough that he does find
    Clouds and darkness in their mind;
40   Darkness but half his work will do.
'Tis not enough; he must find quiet too.

5

The man who, in all wishes he does make,
  Does only Nature's counsel take –
That wise and happy man will never fear
45   The evil aspects of the year,
Nor tremble, though two comets should appear;
He does not look in almanacs to see
  Whether he fortunate shall be;
Let Mars and Saturn in the heav'ns conjoin,
50 And what they please against the world design,
  So Jupiter within him shine.

6

If of your pleasures and desires no end be found,
God to your cares and fears will set no bound.
What would content you? Who can tell?
55   Ye fear so much to lose what you have got,
As if you liked it well;
Ye strive for more, as if ye liked it not.
Go, level hills, and fill up seas,
Spare nought that may your wanton fancy please;
60   But trust me, when you' have done all this,
Much will be missing still, and much will be amiss.

'Begin'

Begin, be bold, and venture to be wise;
He who defers this work from day to day,
Does on a river's bank expecting stay,
Till the whole stream which stopped him should be gone,
5   That runs, and as it runs forever will run on.

'Hell', from the *Davideis*, Book 1

Beneath the silent chambers of the earth,
Where the sun's fruitful beams give metals birth,
Where he the growth of fatal gold does see,
Gold which, above, more influence has than he;
5   Beneath the dens where unfledged tempests lie,
And infant winds their tender voices try;
Beneath the mighty ocean's wealthy waves,
Beneath th' eternal fountain of all waves,
Where their vast court the mother-waters keep,
10   And undisturbed by moons in silence sleep,

There is a place deep, wondrous deep, below,
Which genuine night and horror does o'erflow;
No bound controls th' unwearied space, but hell
Endless as those dire pains that in it dwell.

15 Here no dear glimpse of the sun's lovely face,
Strikes through the solid darkness of the place;
No dawning morn does her kind reds display;
One slight, weak beam would here be thought the day.
No gentle stars with their fair gems of light

20 Offend the tyr'annous and unquestioned night.
Here Lucifer, the mighty captive, reigns,
Proud 'midst his woes, and tyrant in his chains;
Once gen'eral of a gilded host of sprites,
Like Hesper, leading forth the spangled nights.

25 But down like lightning, which him strook, he came;
And roared at his first plunge into the flame.
Myriads of spir'its fell wounded round him there;
With dropping lights thick shone the singèd air.
Since when, the dismal solace of their woe

30 Has only been weak mánkind to undo;
Themselves at first against themselves they'exite
(Their dearest conquest, and most proud delight),
And if those mines of secret treason fail,
With open force man's virtue they assail;

35 Unable to corrupt, seek to destroy;
And where their poisons miss, the sword employ.

4. Happiness

The Wish

1

Well then; I now do plainly see
This busy world and I shall ne'er agree;
The very honey of all earthly joy
    Does of all meats the soonest cloy;
5   And they, methinks, deserve my pity,
Who for it can endure the stings,
The crowd, and buzz, and murmurings,
    Of this great hive, the city.

2

Ah, yet, ere I descend to the'grave,
10 May I a small house and large garden have!
And a few friends, and many books, both true,
    Both wise, and both delightful too!
    And, since love ne'er will from me flee,
A mistress moderately fair,
15 And good as guardian angels are,
    Only belov'd, and loving me!

3

O fountains, when in you shall I
Myself, eased of unpeaceful thoughts, espy?
O fields, O woods, when, when shall I be made
20   The happy tenant of your shade?
    Here's the spring-head of pleasure's flood
Here's wealthy Nature's treasury,
Where all the riches lie, that she
    Has coined and stamped for good.

Pride and ambition here,
25   Only in far-fetched metaphors appear;
Here nought but winds can hurtful murmurs scatter,
    And nought but echo flatter.
The gods, when they descended, hither
From heav'n did always choose their way;
30   And therefore we may boldly say,
    That 'tis the way, too, thither.

5

How happy here should I
And one dear she, live and embracing die!
She who is all the world, and can exclude
35   In deserts solitude.
I should have then this only fear,
Lest men, when they my pleasures see,
Should hither throng to live like me,
    And so make a city here.

A Translation out of Virgil, *Georgics*, Book 2

O happy (if his happiness he knows)
The country swain, on whom kind heav'n bestows
At home all riches that wise Nature needs;
Whom the just earth with easy plenty feeds!
5   'Tis true, no morning tide of clients comes,
And fills the painted channels of his rooms,
Adoring the rich figures, as they pass,
In tap'estry wrought, or cut in living brass;
Nor is his wool superfluously dyed
10   With the dear poison of Assyrian pride;
Nor do Arabian perfumes vainly spoil
The native use and sweetness of his oil.

Instead of these, his calm and harmless life,
Free from th' alarms of fear, and storms of strife,
15 Does with substantial blessedness abound,
And the soft wings of Peace cover him round.
Through artless grots the murm'uring waters glide;
Thick trees both against heat and cold provide,
From whence the birds salute him; and his ground
20 With lowing herds and bleating sheep does sound;
And all the rivers, and the forests nigh,
Both food and game, and exercise supply.
Here a well-hardened, active youth we see
Taught the great art of cheerful poverty;
25 Here, in this place alone, there still do shine
Some streaks of love, both human and divine;
From hence Astraea took her flight, and here
Still her last footsteps upon earth appear.
'Tis true, the first desire which does control
30 All the inferior wheels that move my soul,
Is that the Muse me her high priest would make,
Into her holiest scenes of myst'ery take,
And open there to my mind's purgèd eye
Those wonders which to sense the gods deny:
35 How in the moon such change of shapes is found –
The moon, the changing world's eternal bound;
What shakes the solid earth, what strong disease
Dares trouble the firm centre's ancient ease;
What makes the sea retreat, and what advance
40 (Varieties too regular for chance);
What drives the chariot on of winter's light,
And stops the lazy waggon of the night.
But if my dull and frozen blood deny
To send forth spir'its that raise a soul so high;
45 In the next place, let woods and rivers be
My quiet, though unglorious, destiny.
In life's cool vale let my low scene be laid;
Cover me, gods, with Tempe's thickest shade.
Happy the man, I grant, thrice happy he,
50 Who can through gross effects their causes see;

Whose courage from the deeps of knowledge springs,
Nor vainly fears inevitable things;
But does his walk of virtue calmly go
Through all th' alarms of death and hell below.
55   Happy! but, next such conqu'rors, happy they,
Whose humble life lies not in fortune's way.
They, unconcerned, from their safe, distant seat
Behold the rods and sceptres of the great;
The quarrels of the mighty without fear,
60 And the descent of foreign troops they hear;
Nor can ev'n Rome their steady course misguide,
With all the lustre of her per'ishing pride.
Them never yet did strife or av'arice draw
Into the noisy markets of the Law,
65 The camps of gownèd war; nor do they live
By rules or forms that many madmen give.
Duty for Nature's bounty they repay,
And her sole laws religiously obey.
    Some with bold labour plough the faithless main,
70 Some rougher storms in princes' courts sustain;
Some swell up their slight sails with pop'ular fame,
Charmed with the foolish whistlings of a name;
Some their vain wealth to earth again commit;
With endless cares some brooding o'er it sit;
75 Country and friends are by some wretches sold,
To lie on Tyrian beds and drink in gold;
No price too high for profit can be shown;
Not brothers' blood, nor hazards of their own;
Around the world in search of it they roam;
80 It makes ev'n their antipodes their home;
Meanwhile, the prudent husbandman is found
In mutual duties striving with his ground,
And half the year he care of that does take,
That half the year grateful returns does make.
85 Each fertile month does some new gifts present,
And with new work his industry content.
This the young lamb, that the soft fleece, doth yield;
This loads with hay, and that with corn, the field;

All sorts of fruit crown the rich autumn's pride;
90   And on a swelling hill's warm stony side,
The powerful princely purple of the vine,
Twice dyed with the redoubled sun does shine.
In th' evening to a fair ensuing day
With joy he sees his flocks and kids to play;
95   And loaded kine about his cottage stand,
Inviting with known sound the milker's hand;
And when from wholesome labour he doth come,
With wishes to be there, and wished-for home,
He meets at door the softest human blisses,
100   His chaste wife's welcome, and dear children's kisses.
When any rural holidays invite
His genius forth to innocent delight,
On earth's fair bed, beneath some sacred shade,
Amidst his equal friends carelessly laid,
105   He sings thee, Bacchus, patron of the vine;
The beechen bowl foams with a flood of wine,
Not to the loss of reason or of strength;
To active games and manly sport at length
Their mirth ascends, and with filled veins they see
110   Who can the best at better trials be.
    Such was the life the prudent Sabines chose;
From such the old Etrurian virtue rose;
Such Remus and the god his brother led;
From such firm footing Rome grew the world's head.
115   Such was the life that, ev'n till now, does raise
The honour of poor Saturn's golden days;
Before men, born of earth, and buried there,
Let in the sea their mortal fate to share;
Before new ways of perishing were sought;
120   Before unskilful death on anvils wrought;
Before those beasts which human life sustain,
By men, unless to the gods' use, were slain.

Horace : Epode 2

Happy the man, whom bounteous gods allow
With his own hands paternal grounds to plough!
Like the first golden mortals happy he,
From business and the cares of money free!
No human storms break off at land his sleep;
No loud alarms of nature on the deep;
From all the cheats of law he lives secure;
Nor does th' affronts of palaces endure;
Sometimes the beauteous, marriageable vine
He to the lusty bridegroom-elm does join;
Sometimes he lops the barren trees around,
And grafts new life into the fruitful wound;
Sometimes he shears his flock, and sometimes he
Stores up the golden treasures of the bee.
He sees his lowing herds walk o'er the plain,
Whilst neighb'ring hills low back to them again;
And when the season, rich as well as gay,
All her autumnal bounty does display,
How is he pleased th' increasing use to see
Of his well-trusted labours bend the tree!
Of which large shares, on the glad sacred days,
He gives to friends, and to the gods repays.
With how much joy does he, beneath some shade
By agèd trees' rev'rend embraces made,
His careless head on the fresh green recline,
His head uncharged with fear or with design!
By him a river constantly complains,
The birds above rejoice with various strains,
And in the solemn scene their orgies keep,
Like dreams mixed with the gravity of sleep;
Sleep, which does always there for entrance wait,
And nought within against it shuts the gate.
  Nor does the roughest season of the sky,
Or sullen Jove, all sports to him deny;
He runs the mazes of the nimble hare,
His well-mouthed dogs' glad concert rends the air,

Or with game bolder, and rewarded more,
He drives into a toil the foaming boar;
Here flies the hawk to'assault, and there the net
40   To intercept the trav'elling fowl is set;
And all his malice, all his craft, is shown
In inn'ocent wars on beasts and birds alone.
This is the life from all misfortunes free,
From thee, the great one, tyrant Love, from thee;
45   And if a chaste and clean, though homely, wife
Be added to the blessings of this life
(Such as the ancient, sunburnt Sabines were,
Such as Apulia, frugal still, does bear),
Who makes her children and the house her care,
50   And joyfully the work of life does share,
Nor thinks herself too noble or too fine
To pin the sheepfold, or to milk the kine;
Who waits at door against her husband come
From rural duties, late and wearied, home,
55   Where she receives him with a kind embrace,
A cheerful fire, and a more cheerful face;
And fills the bowl up to her homely lord,
And with domestic plenty loads the board.
Not all the lustful shellfish of the sea,
60   Dressed by the wanton hand of Luxury,
Nor ortolans, nor godwits, nor the rest
Of costly names that glorify a feast,
Are at the princely tables better cheer
Than lamb and kid, lettuce and olives, here.

The Country Mouse
A Paraphrase upon Horace, Book 2, Satire 6

At the large foot of a fair hollow tree,
Close to ploughed ground, seated commodiously,
His ancient and hereditary house,
There dwelt a good, substantial country mouse;
5   Frugal and grave, and careful of the main,
Yet one who once did nobly entertain
A city mouse, well-coated, sleek and gay,
A mouse of high degree, which lost his way,
Wantonly walking forth to take the air,
10   And arrived early, and belighted, there
For a day's lodging. The good hearty host
(The ancient plenty of his hall to boast)
Did all the stores produce that might excite,
With various tastes, the courtier's appetite:
15   Fitches and beans, peason, and oats and wheat,
And a large chestnut, the delicious meat
Which Jove himself, were he a mouse, would eat.
And for a *hautgoust* there was mixed with these
The swerd of bacon and the coat of cheese:
20   The precious relics, which at harvest he
Had gathered from the reapers' luxury.
'Freely,' said he, 'fall on, and never spare!
The bounteous gods will for tomorrow care!'
And thus at ease on beds of straw they lay,
25   And to their genius sacrificed the day.
    Yet the nice guest's epicurean mind
(Though breeding made him civil seem, and kind)
Despised this country feast, and still his thought
Upon the cakes and pies of London wrought.
30   'Your bounty and civility,' said he,
'Which I'm surprised in these rude parts to see,
Shows that the gods have given you a mind
Too noble for the fate which here you find.
Why should a soul so virt'uous and so great
35   Lose itself thus in an obscure retreat?

Let savage beasts lodge in a country den;
You should see towns, and manners know, and men,
And taste the gen'rous luxury of the court,
Where all the mice of quality resort;
40   Where thousand beauteous shes about you move,
And by high fare are pliant made to love.
We all ere long must render up our breath;
No cave or hole can shelter us from death.
Since life is so uncertain and so short,
45   Let's spend it all in feasting and in sport;
Come, worthy sir, come with me, and partake
All the great things that mortals happy make!'
    Alas, what virtue hath sufficient arms
To'oppose bright honour and soft pleasure's charms?
50   What wisdom can their magic force repel?
It draws the rev'rend hermit from his cell.
It was the time when witty poets tell
'That Phoebus into Thetis' bosom fell;
She blushed at first, and then put out the light,
55   And drew the modest curtains of the night.'
Plainly the truth to tell, the sun was set,
When to the town our wearied travellers get.
To a lord's house, as lordly as can be,
Made for the use of Pride and Luxury,
60   They come; the gentle courtier at the door
Stops, and will hardly enter in before –
'But 'tis, sir, your command, and, being so,
I'm sworn to'obedience' – and so, in they go.
    Behind a hanging in a spacious room
65   (The richest work of Mortlake's noble loom)
They wait a while, their wearied limbs to rest,
Till silence should invite them to their feast;
'About the hour that Cynthia's silver light
Had touched the pale *meridies* of the night.'
70   At last, the various supper being done,
It happened that the company was gone
Into a room remote, servants and all,
To please their nobles' fancies with a ball.

Our host leads forth his stranger, and does find
75   All fitted to the bounties of his mind.
Still on the table half-filled dishes stood,
And with delicious bits the floor was strewed.
The courteous mouse presents him with the best,
And both with fat varieties are blessed.
80   Th' industrious peasant everywhere does range,
And thanks the gods for his life's happy change.
      Lo, in the midst of a well-freighted pie
They both at last glutted and wanton lie!
When see the sad reverse of prosp'rous Fate,
85   And what fierce storms on mortal glories wait!
With hideous noise down the rude servants come;
Six dogs before run barking into the' room;
The wretched gluttons fly with wild affright,
And hate the fullness which retards their flight.
90   Our trembling peasant wishes now in vain
That rocks and mountains covered him again.
O, how the change of his poor life he cursed:
'This, of all lives,' said he, 'is sure the worst!
Give me again, ye gods, my cave and wood;
95   With peace, let tares and acorns be my food!'

Claudian's Old Man of Verona

Happy the man, who his whole time doth bound
Within th' enclosure of his little ground.
Happy the man, whom the same humble place
(Th' hereditary cottage of his race)
5   From his first rising infancy has known,
And by degrees sees gently bending down,
With natural propension to that earth
Which both preserved his life and gave him birth.
Him no false distant lights, by fortune set,
10   Could ever into foolish wand'rings get.

He never dangers either saw or feared;
The dreadful storms at sea he never heard.
He never heard the shrill alarms of war,
Or the worse noises of the lawyers' Bar.
15 No change of consuls marks to him the year;
The change of seasons is his calendar.
The cold and heat, winter and summer shows;
Autumn by fruits, and spring by flow'rs he knows.
He measures time by landmarks, and has found
20 For the whole day the dial of his ground.
A neighb'ring wood born with himself he sees,
And loves his old contemporary trees.
He has only heard of near Verona's name,
And knows it like the Indies, but by fame;
25 Does with a like concernment notice take
Of the Red Sea and of Benacus' lake.
Thus health and strength he to a third age enjoys,
And sees a long posterity of boys.
About the spacious world let others roam;
30 The voyage life is longest made at home.

The Complaint

1

In a deep vision's intellectual scene,
Beneath a bow'r for sorrow made,
Th' uncomfortable shade
Of the black yew's unlucky green,
5 Mixed with the mourning willow's careful grey,
Where rev'rend Cam cuts out his famous way,
The melancholy Cowley lay;
And lo, a Muse appeared to his closed sight
(The Muses oft in lands of vision play),
10 Bodied, arrayed, and seen, by an internal light.
A golden harp with silver strings she bore;

60

A wondrous hieroglyphic robe she wore,
In which all colours and all figures were,
That nature or that fancy can create,
15   That art can never imitate;
And with loose pride it wantoned in the air.
In such a dress, in such a well-clothed dream,
She used of old, near fair Ismenus' stream,
Pindar, her Theban favourite, to meet;
20   A crown was on her head, and wings were on her feet.

2

She touched him with her harp, and raised him from
                                        the ground;
The shaken strings melodiously resound.
      'Art thou returned at last,' said she,
      'To this forsaken place and me?
25   Thou prodigal, who didst so loosely waste
Of all thy youthful years the good estate;
Art thou returned here, to repent too late,
And gather husks of learning up at last,
Now the rich harvest-time of life is past,
30   And winter marches on so fast?
But when I meant to'adopt thee for my son,
And did as learn'd a portion assign,
As ever any of the mighty Nine
      Had to their dearest children done;
35   When I resolved to'exalt thy'anointed name
Among the spir'itual lords of peaceful fame,
Thou changeling, thou, bewitched with noise and show
Wouldst into courts and cities from me go!
Wouldst see the world abroad, and have a share
40   In all the follies and the tumults there!
Thou wouldst, forsooth, be something in a state,
And business thou wouldst find, and wouldst create;
      Business, the frivolous pretence
Of human lusts, to shake off innocence!
45   Business, the grave impertinence!

Business, the thing which I of all things hate!
Business, the contradiction of thy fate!

3

Go, renegado, cast up thy account,
   And see to what amount
50   Thy foolish gains by quitting me:
The sale of knowledge, fame, and liberty,
The fruits of thy unlearn'd apostasy.
Thou thought'st, if once the public storm was past,
All thy remaining life should sunshine be;
55 Behold, the public storm is spent at last,
   The Sov'reign's tossed at sea no more,
And thou, with all the noble company,
   Art got at last to shore.
But whilst thy fellow-voyagers I see
60 All marched up to possess the promised land,
Thou still alone, alas, dost gaping stand
Upon the naked beach, upon the barren sand!

4

As a fair morning of the blessèd spring,
   After a tedious, stormy night,
65 Such was the glorious entry of our king;
Enriching moisture dropped on everything;
Plenty he sowed below, and cast about him light!
   But then, alas, to thee alone
One of old Gideon's miracles was shown;
70 For ev'ry tree and ev'ry herb around
   With pearly dew was crowned,
   And upon all the quickened ground
The fruitful seed of heav'n did brooding lie,
And nothing but the Muse's fleece was dry.
75   It did all other threats surpass,
   When God to His own people said
(The men whom through long wand'rings he had led)

That He would give them ev'n a heav'n of brass;
  They looked up to that heav'n in vain,
That bounteous heav'n, which God did not restrain,
Upon the most unjust to shine and rain.

5

The Rachel, for which twice sev'n years and more
  Thou didst with faith and labour serve,
  And didst (if faith and labour can) deserve,
    Though she contracted was to thee,
    Giv'n to another thou didst see;
    Giv'n to another, who had store
  Of fairer and of richer wives before,
And not a Leah left, thy recompense to be!
  Go on: twice sev'n years more thy fortune try;
  Twice sev'n years more God in His bounty may
    Give thee, to fling away
  Into the court's deceitful lottery;
    But think how likely 'tis that thou,
  With the dull work of thy unwieldy plough,
Shouldst in a hard and barren season thrive,
    Shouldst even able be to live;
  Thou, to whose share so little bread did fall,
In the mirac'ulous year when manna rained on all.'

6

Thus spake the Muse, and spake it with a smile,
  That seemed at once to pity and revile;
  And to her thus, raising his thoughtful head,
    The melancholy Cowley said,
    'Ah, wanton foe, dost thou upbraid
    The ills which thou thyself hast made?
When in the cradle innocent I lay,
Thou, wicked spirit, stolest me away,
    And my abusèd soul didst bear
Into thy new-found worlds, I know not where,

110   Thy golden Indies in the air;
     And ever since I strive in vain
     My ravished freedom to regain;
     Still I rebel, still thou dost reign;
     Lo, still in verse against thee I complain.
115   There is a sort of stubborn weeds,
     Which, if the earth but once, it ever breeds;
     No wholesome herb can near them thrive;
     No useful plant can keep alive;
     The foolish sports I did on thee bestow,
120   Make all my art and labour fruitless now;
     Where once such fairies dance, no grass doth ever grow.

7

     When my new mind had no infusion known,
     Thou gav'st so deep a tincture of thine own,
     That ever since I vainly try
125   To wash away th' inherent dye;
     Long work perhaps may spoil thy colours quite,
     But never will reduce the native white;
     To all the ports of honour and of gain
     I often steer my course in vain;
130   Thy gale comes cross, and drives me back again.
     Thou slack'nest all my nerves of industry,
     By making them so oft to be
     The tinkling strings of thy loose minstrelsy.
     Whoever this world's happiness would see,
135   Must as entirely cast off thee
     As they who only heav'n desire
     Do from the world retire.
     This was my error, this my gross mistake,
     Myself a demi-votary to make.
140   Thus with Sapphira and her husband's fate
     (A fault which I, like them, am taught too late),
     For all that I gave up I nothing gain,
     And perish for the part which I retain.

8

Teach me not then, O thou fallacious Muse,
145   The court and better king to'accuse;
The heaven under which I live is fair,
The fertile soil will a full harvest bear;
Thine, thine is all the barrenness, if thou
Mak'st me sit still and sing, when I should plough.
150 When I but think how many'a tedious year
   Our patient Sov'reign did attend
   His long misfortune's fatal end;
How cheerfully, and how exempt from fear,
On the Great Sov'reign's will he did depend;
155 I ought to be accursed if I refuse
To wait on his, O thou fallacious Muse!
Kings have long hands, they say, and though I be
So distant, they may reach at length to me.
   However, of all princes, thou
160 Shouldst not reproach rewards for being small or slow;
   Thou who rewardest but with pop'ular breath,
     And that, too, after death.

In Imitation of Martial's Epigram (Book 5, Epigram 20)

If, dearest friend, it my good fate might be
To'enjoy at once a quiet life and thee;
If we for happiness could leisure find,
And wand'ring time into a method bind,
5 We should not, sure, the great men's favour need,
Nor on long hopes, the court's thin diet, feed.
We should not patience find daily to hear
The calumnies and flatt'ries spoken there;
We should not the lords' tables humbly use,
10 Or talk in ladies' chambers love and news;
But books, and wise discourse, gardens and fields,

And all the joys that unmixed nature yields;
Thick summer shades where winter still does lie;
Bright winter fires that summer's part supply;
15 Sleep not controlled by cares, confined to night,
Or bound in any rule but appetite;
Free, but not savage or ungracious mirth;
Rich wines to give it quick and easy birth;
A few companions, which ourselves should choose,
20 A gentle mistress, and a gentler Muse.
Such, dearest friend, such without doubt should be
Our place, our business, and our company.
Now to himself, alas, does neither live,
But sees good suns, of which we are to give
25 A strict account, set and march thick away;
Knows a man how to live, and does he stay?

5. On Poetry

The Muse

1

Go, the rich chariot instantly prepare;
   The Queen, my Muse, will take the air;
Unruly Fancy with strong Judgement trace,
   Put in nimble-footed Wit,
     Smooth-paced El'oquence join with it,
Sound Memory with young Invention place,
   Harness all the wingèd race.
Let the postilion Nature mount, and let
   The coachman Art be set.
And let the airy footmen, running all beside,
   Make a long row of goodly pride.
Figures, Conceits, Raptures, and Sentences,
   In a well-worded dress.
And inn'ocent Loves, and pleasant Truths, and useful
                           Lies,
   In all their gaudy liveries.
Mount, glorious Queen, thy trav'elling throne,
   And bid it to put on;
For long, though cheerful, is the way,
And life, alas, allows but one ill winter's day.

2

Where never foot of man, or hoof of beast
   The passage pressed,
   Where never fish did fly,
And with short silver wings cut the low, liquid sky.
   Where bird with painted oars did ne'er
   Row through the trackless ocean of the air.
   Where never yet did pry

The busy Morning's curious eye,
The wheels of thy bold coach pass quick and free,
And all's an open road to thee.
30   Whatever God did say,
Is all thy plain and smooth, uninterrupted way.
Nay ev'n beyond His works thy voyages are known,
Thou'st thousand worlds, too, of thine own.
Thou speak'st, great Queen, in the same style as He,
35   And a new world leaps forth when thou say'st, 'Let it be.'

3

Thou fathom'st the deep gulf of ages past,
And canst pluck up with ease
The years which thou dost please,
Like shipwrecked treasures by rude tempests cast
40   Long since into the sea,
Brought up again to light and public use by thee.
Nor dost thou only dive so low,
But fly
With an unwearied wing the other way on high,
45   Where Fates among the stars do grow;
There into the close nests of time dost peep,
And there with piercing eye,
Through the firm shell and the thick white dost spy,
Years to come a-forming lie,
50   Close in their sacred secondine asleep,
Till hatched by the sun's vital heat
Which o'er them yet does brooding set
They life and motion get,
And ripe at last with vig'orous might
55   Break through the shell, and take their everlasting flight.

4

And sure we may
The same too of the present say,
If past and future times do thee obey.

Thou stop'st this current, and dost make
60   This running river settle like a lake;
Thy certain hand holds fast this slipp'ry snake.
    The fruit which does so quickly waste,
    Men scarce can see it, much less taste,
Thou comfitest in sweets, to make it last.
65   This shining piece of ice
            Which melts so soon away
              With the sun's ray,
Thy verse does solidate and crystallize,
Till it a lasting mirror be.
70   Nay, thy immortal rhyme
        Makes this one short point of time
To fill up half the orb of round eternity.

The Praise of Pindar
In Imitation of Horace's Second Ode, Book 4

1

Pindar is im'itable by none;
The phoenix Pindar is a vast species alone.
Whoe'er but Daedalus with waxen wings could fly,
    And neither sink too low nor soar too high?
5   What could he who followed claim,
    But of vain boldness the unhappy fame,
        And by his fall a sea to name?
        Pindar's unnavigable song
Like a swoll'n flood from some steep mountain pours
                                              along;
10   The ocean meets with such a voice,
From his enlargèd mouth, as drowns the ocean's noise.

2

So Pindar does new words and figures roll
Down his impetuous dithyrambic tide,
  Which in no channel deigns to'abide,
15   Which neither banks nor dykes control;
  Whether th' immortal gods he sings,
  In a no less immortal strain,
Or the great acts of god-descended kings,
Who in his numbers still survive and reign;
20   Each rich-embroidered line,
  Which their triumphant brows around
  By his sacred hand is bound,
Does all their starry diadems outshine.

3

Whether at Pisa's race he please
25 To carve in polished verse the conqu'ror's images;
  Whether the swift, the skilful, or the strong,
Be crownèd in his nimble, artful, vig'orous song;
  Whether some brave young man's untimely fate
  In words worth dying for he celebrate
30   (Such mournful and such pleasing words,
As joy to'his mother's and his mistress' grief affords),
  He bids him live and grow in fame;
  Among the stars he sticks his name;
  The grave can but the dross of him devour,
35 So small is death's, so great the poet's power!

4

Lo, how th' obsequious wind, and swelling air,
The Theban swan does upwards bear
Into the walks of clouds, where he does play,
And with extended wings opens his liquid way!
40   Whilst, alas, my tim'orous Muse
  Unambitious tracks pursues;
  Does with weak, unballassed wings,

About the mossy brooks and springs,
About the trees' new-blossomed heads,
45 About the gardens' painted beds,
About the fields and flow'ry meads,
And all inferior beauteous things,
  Like the laborious bee,
For little drops of honey flee,
50 And there with humble sweets contents her industry.

The Resurrection

1

Not winds to voyagers at sea,
Nor show'rs to earth more necessary be
(Heav'ns vital seed cast on the womb of earth
  To give the fruitful year a birth)
5   Than verse to virtue, which does do
The midwife's office and the nurse's too;
It feeds it strongly, and it clothes it gay,
  And when it dies, with comely pride
Embalms it, and erects a pyramid
10   That never will decay
  Till heav'n itself shall melt away,
    And nought behind it stay.

2

Begin the song, and strike the living lyre;
Lo, how the years to come, a num'rous and well-fitted
choir,
15   All hand in hand do decently advance,
And to my song with smooth and equal measures dance.
  Whilst the dance lasts, how long soe'er it be,
  My music's voice shall bear it company.
    Till all gentle notes be drowned

In the last trumpet's dreadful sound.
That to the spheres themselves shall silence bring,
Untune the universal string;
Then all the wide-extended sky,
And all th' harmonious worlds on high,
And Virgil's sacred work shall die;
And he himself shall see in one fire shine
Rich nature's ancient Troy, though built by hands divine.

3

Whom thunder's dismal noise,
And all that prophets and apostles louder spake,
And all the creatures' plain conspiring voice,
Could not, whilst they lived, awake,
This mightier sound shall make
When dead to'arise;
And open tombs, and open eyes,
To the long sluggards of five thousand years.
This mightier sound shall make its hearers ears.
Then shall the scattered atoms crowding come
Back to their ancient home;
Some from birds, from fishes some;
Some from earth, and some from seas;
Some from beasts, and some from trees;
Some descend from clouds on high,
Some from metals upwards fly,
And where th' attending soul naked, and shivering
stands,
Meet, salute, and join their hands;
As dispersed soldiers, at the trumpet's call,
Haste to their colours all.
Unhappy most, like tortured men,
Their joints new-set, to be new-racked again,
To mountains they for shelter pray,
The mountains shake, and run about no less confused
than they.

Stop, stop, my Muse, allay thy vig'orous heat,
    Kindled at a hint so great;
Hold thy Pindaric Peg'asus closely in,
55   Which does to rage begin,
And this steep hill would gallop up with violent course;
  'Tis an unruly and a hard-mouthed horse,
    Fierce and unbroken yet,
    Impatient of the spur or bit;
60 Now prances stately, and anon flies o'er the place;
Disdains the servile law of any settled place,
  Conscious and proud of his own nat'ural force.
   'Twill no unskilful touch endure,
But flings writer and reader too, that sits not sure.

Destiny

Hoc quoque fatale est sic ipsum expendere fatum.
(Manilius)

1

Strange and unnatural! let's stay and see
    This pageant of a prodigy.
Lo, of themselves th' enlivened chessmen move,
Lo, the unbred, ill-organed pieces prove
5   As full of art and industry,
    Of courage and of policy,
As we ourselves, who think there's nothing wise but we.
     Here a proud pawn I'admire
     That still advancing higher
10   At top of all became
     Another thing and name;
Here I'm amazed at th' actions of a knight
   That does bold wonders in the fight;
   Here I the losing party blame

73

15   For those false moves that break the game,
    That to their grave, the bag, the conquered pieces bring,
    And above all th' ill conduct of the mated king.

       2
    'Whate'er these seem, whate'er philosophy
     And sense or reason tell,' said I,
20   'These things have life, election, liberty;
     'Tis their own wisdom moulds their state,
     Their faults and virtues make their fate.
     They do, they do,' said I; but straight
  Lo from my'enlightened eyes the mists and shadows fell,
25   That hinder spir'its from being visible.
    And, lo! I saw two angels played the mate.
    With man, alas, no otherwise it proves;
     An unseen hand makes all their moves.
     And some are great, and some are small,
30   Some climb to good, some from good fortune fall,
     Some wise men and some fools we call –
  Figures, alas, of speech! Destiny plays us all.

       3
    Me from the womb the midwife Muse did take;
    She cut my navel, washed me, and mine head
35   With her own hands she fashionèd;
     She did a cov'enant with me make,
  And circumcised my tender soul, and thus she spake:
     'Thou of my church shalt be;
     Hate and renounce,' said she,
40   'Wealth, honour, pleasures, all the world, for me.
    Thou neither great at court, nor in the war,
  Nor at th' Exchange shalt be, nor at the wrangling Bar.
    Content thyself with the small, barren praise
     That neglected verse does raise.'
45   She spake, and all my years to come
     Took their unlucky doom.

Their sev'ral ways of life let others choose,
   Their sev'ral pleasures let them use;
But I was born for love, and for a Muse.

4

50   With Fate what boots it to contend?
   Such I began, such am, and so must end.
      The star that did my being frame
         Was but a lambent flame,
      And some small light it did dispense,
55   But neither heat nor influence.
   No matter, Cowley! let proud Fortune see
That thou canst her despise no less than she does thee.
      Let all her gifts the portion be
      Of Folly, Lust, and Flattery,
60   Fraud, Extortion, Calumny,
         Murder, Infidelity,
      Rebellion and Hypocrisy.
      Do thou not grieve nor blush to be
      As all th' inspirèd tuneful men,
65   And all thy great forefathers were from Homer down to
                                          Ben.

Ode: Of Wit

1

Tell me, O tell, what kind of thing is wit,
   Thou who master art of it.
For the first matter loves vari'ety less,
Less women love'it, either in love or dress.
5   A thousand diff'rent shapes it bears,
         Comely in thousand shapes appears.
Yonder we saw it plain; and here 'tis now,
Like spirits in a place, we know not how.

London, that vents of false ware so much store,
10   In no ware deceives us more;
For men, led by the colour and the shape,
Like Zeuxis' birds fly to the painted grape;
    Some things do through our judgement pass
    As through a multiplying glass.
15 And sometimes, if the object be too far,
We take a falling meteor for a star.

3

Hence 'tis a wit, that greatest word of fame,
    Grows such a common name;
And wits by our creation they become,
20 Just so as tit'ular bishops made at Rome.
    'Tis not a tale, 'tis not a jest
    Admired with laughter at a feast,
Nor florid talk which can that title gain;
The proofs of wit for ever must remain.

4

25 'Tis not to force some lifeless verses meet
    With their five gouty feet.
All everywhere, like man's, must be the soul,
And reason the inferior powers control.
    Such were the numbers which could call
30   The stones into the Theban wall.
Such miracles are ceased; and now we see
No towns or houses raised by poetry.

5

Yet 'tis not to adorn and gild each part;
    That shows more cost than art.
35 Jewels at nose and lips but ill appear;
Rather than all things wit, let none be there.

Sev'ral lights will not be seen,
If there be nothing else between.
Men doubt, because they stand so thick i' th' sky,
40   If those be stars which paint the galaxy.

6

'Tis not when two like words make up one noise,
    Jests for Dutch men and English boys;
In which who finds out wit, the same may see
In an'agrams and acrostics poetry.
45   Much less can that have any place
        At which a virgin hides her face;
Such dross the fire must purge away; 'tis just
The author blush there, where the reader must.

7

'Tis not such lines as almost crack the stage
50   When Bajazet begins to rage;
Nor a tall metaphor in th' Oxford way,
Nor the dry chips of short-lunged Seneca;
        Nor upon all things to obtrude,
        And force some odd similitude.
55 What is it, then, which like the Pow'r Divine
We only can by negatives define?

8

In a true piece of wit all things must be,
    Yet all things there agree.
As in the ark, joined without force or strife,
60 All creatures dwelt; all creatures that had life.
        Or as the prim'itive forms of all
        (If we compare great things with small)
Which without discord or confusion lie,
In that strange mirror of the Deity.

65 But Love that moulds one man up out of two,
    Makes me forget and injure you.
  I took you for myself, sure, when I thought
  That you in any thing were to be taught.
    Correct my error with thy pen;
70   And if any ask me then,
  What thing right wit, and height of genius is,
  I'll only show your lines, and say, ''Tis this.'

'The Music of Creation', from the *Davideis*, Book 1

  As first a various, unformed hint we find
  Rise in some godlike poet's fertile mind,
  Till all the parts and words their places take,
  And with just marches verse and music make;
5 Such was God's poem, this world's new essay;
  So wild and rude in its first draft it lay;
  Th' ungoverned parts no correspondence knew,
  An artless war from thwarting motions grew,
  Till they to number and fixed rules were brought
10 By the Eternal Mind's poetic thought.
  Water and air he for the tenor chose,
  Earth made the bass, the treble flame arose,
  To th' active moon a quick, brisk stroke he gave,
  To Saturn's string a touch more soft and grave;
15 The motions straight, and round, and swift, and slow,
  And short, and long, were mixed and woven so,
  Did in such artful figures smoothly fall,
  As made this decent, measured dance of all.
  And this is music; sounds that charm our ears
20 Is but one dressing that rich science wears.
  Though no man hear'it, though no man it rehearse,
  Yet will there still be music in my verse.

In this great world so much of it we see;
The lesser, man, is all-o'er harmony.
Storehouse of all proportions! Single choir!
Which first God's breath did tunefully inspire!
From hence blest music's heav'nly charms arise,
From sympathy which them and man allies.

25

Notes

The following abbreviations are used below to indicate the volume in which each poem was first published:

  1647: *The Mistress* (unauthorized edition, 1647)
  1656: *Poems* (1656)
  1663: *Verses Written upon Several Occasions* (1663)
  1668: *The Works of Mr Abraham Cowley*, ed. Thomas Sprat (1668)

C = Cowley's own note

For further information on the texts and contexts of Cowley's work, and for comprehensive listings of secondary material on the poet, readers are referred to the excellent, fully-annotated, library edition of *The Collected Works of Abraham Cowley* (edited by Thomas O. Calhoun, Laurence Heyworth, Robert B. Hinman, William B. Hunter, Allan Pritchard, and Ernest W. Sullivan II), currently being published by the University of Delaware Press (6 volumes projected; Vols. 1 (1989) and 2, Part 1 (1993) published so far).

(pp. 1-9) *Anacreontics* *(1656)* The poems are free adaptations from the *Anacreontea*, a collection of Greek verse thought in Cowley's day to be the work of Anacreon (*c.* 570-485 B.C.), but now known to be by various authors, and to date mainly from the late Hellenistic and early Roman periods. A 'Life of Anacreon' had come down from antiquity, in which the poet was depicted as a lifelong devotee of love and wine, who had died in his eighty-fifth year by choking on a grape stone.

(p. 1) *1. Love*
2   *mighty numbers* high-flown verse, sounding versification
17   *just to* in a way that harmonizes perfectly with
(p. 2) *3. Beauty*
23   *Cap-à-pie* from head to foot
(p. 3) *4. The Duel*
7   *Ajax* after Achilles, the strongest and bravest of the Greeks fighting at Troy
8   *Love* i.e. Cupid, the boy-god of love
9   *dart* spear
21   *work* fortification
(p. 4) *5. Age*
11   *stake* wager (e.g. in a game of dice)

81

(p. 4) 6. *The Account*

1	*told* totalled up
29	*Xerxes* King Xerxes led the vast Persian forces which invaded Greece in 480 B.C., and which included many contingents from allied nations (described at length by Herodotus, *Histories* 7.61-99).
42	*the line* the Equator

(p. 6) 8. *The Epicure*

Title	*Epicure* See poem 10, note on l. 32.
6	*Gyges' wealthy diadem* According to Plato (*Republic* 2. 359-60), the shepherd Gyges discovered a magic ring which enabled him to usurp the throne of Lydia.

(p. 6) 9. *Another*

2	*supinely* flat on my back
27	*Stoics* The Stoic philosophers advocated cultivating a resolute indifference to all human pleasures and pains.

(p. 7) 10. *The Grasshopper*

8	*Nature self's* i.e. Nature herself is
	Ganymede cup-bearer to Zeus
18	*luxury* indulgence in pleasure
21	*hinds* labourers
23	*Phoebus* Apollo, the sun god
25-6	The grasshopper only lives for a few, short, summer months.
32	*Epicurean* Though the Epicurean philosophers were popularly associated with mindless and profligate hedonism, the teachings of Epicurus (341-270 B.C.) actually advocated the attainment of *ataraxia* (freedom from worldly anxiety) via the cultivation of life's simplest pleasures.

(p. 8) 11. *The Swallow*

4-5	Tereus, King of Thrace, raped Philomela and cut out her tongue so that she could not expose his villainy. In the myth, Philomela was subsequently metamorphosed into a nightingale.

(p. 9) *Elegy upon Anacreon* (1656)

Title	*the god of love* Cupid
14	*my mother's* Venus'
18	*Venus' girdle* Venus' *cestus* or love-girdle, a magic charm which inspired instant passion in the beholder
22	*num'rously* (i) rapidly (ii) poetically

36	*like Meleager's fate* Meleager died when his mother, in a fit of anger over the death of her brothers, plunged into the fire a brand of wood, on the preservation of which (the Fates had decreed) her son's life depended.
37	*antiperistasis* force or effect working in a diametrically opposite, or sharply contrasted, way to that which you would expect (see Introduction, p. xvii)
46	*idea* model, archetype
86-8	Plutarch (*Isis and Osiris* 6) records this as an Egyptian belief.
114	*aconite* deadly poison

p. 12 *The Chronicle: A Ballad* (1656) For the title, see note to l. 78.

4	*wanton* sportive, capricious
14	*evil counsels* It was a regular charge in seventeenth-century political polemic that the writer's opponents had been corrupted by malign counsellors. The speaker of this poem plays throughout on analogies between political and historical events and language and the course of his love-affairs.
15	*Fundamental laws* essential and indispensable laws which must not be broken. Both sides in the English Civil War claimed that their opponents had breached 'fundamental laws'.
16	*still* continuously
	favourites (i) lovers (ii) courtiers favoured by a king
50	*viceroy-maid* Bess now 'rules' in lieu of her mistress.
51	*To* After
	vacancy period with no-one holding office
53	*interregnum* (alluding to the period between the execution of Charles I (1649) and the restoration of the monarchy hoped for by royalists)
54	*anarchy* (i) moral disorder (ii) rule without a monarch
55	*then* ('than' in the 1656 text)
63	*patches* black cosmetic patches, worn on the face
66	*magazines* (i) wardrobes (ii) weaponries
72	*mysteries* (i) puzzles (ii) religious marvels
73	*lime-twigs* (used to trap birds)
74	*Matchavil* i.e. Machiavelli; the Florentine writer (1459-1517) was popularly renowned for his advocacy of amoral political strategy.
78	*Holinshed or Stow* Raphael Holinshed's *Chronicles* (1577)

and John Stow's *Chronicles of England* (1580) were encyclo-
pedic historical works, which catalogued the circum-
stances surrounding major events (including storms,
droughts, etc.) in great detail.

(p. 16) ***Ode: Acme and Septimius*** *(1668)* A free translation of Catullus,
Poem 45.

16	*Sneezed* (a lucky omen)
17	*Loves* Cupids, love gods

(p. 18) ***Ode: In Imitation of Horace his Ode [Book 1, Ode 5]*** *(1656)*

1	*kind* amorously indulgent
4	*sweets* pleasures, delights
6	*cabinet* (i) boudoir (ii) jewel-case
8	*changed faith* unreliable promises (with a play on 'altered religion')
10	*vain* worthless
11	*chameleon-like* The chameleon is able to change the colour of its skin and was allegedly capable of living on air.
12	*still* constantly
	it i.e. Pyrrha's 'faith'
13	*admire* marvel at, stand in awe of
24	*April* (proverbially associated in England with unreliable weather)
27	*untried* untested (and therefore not yet found unreliable)
29	*Loreto's shrine* the Santa Casa, the shrine to the Virgin Mary at Loreto (see 'On the Death of Mr Crashaw', ll. 39-46); it was the custom for sailors to hang model boats in the shrine as a thanks-offering for having arrived safely ashore.

(p. 20) Brutus *(1656)*

1	*Brutus* Marcus Junius Brutus (?85-42 B.C.), a Roman patrician renowned for his studiousness and moral probity, was one of those who conspired to assassinate Julius Caesar in 44 B.C.. After Caesar's death, Brutus' and Cassius' forces were defeated by those of Mark Antony and Octavian at the battle of Philippi, and Brutus subsequently took his own life. In the seventeenth century, Brutus was renowned as a republican tyranni-cide, and Cowley's poem was thus suspected of revealing its author's secret sympathy with, or appeasement of,

the Cromwellian party (see A.H. Nethercot, *Abraham Cowley: The Muses' Hannibal* (Oxford, 1931), pp. 153, 199-200). But Brutus was also seen as an exemplar of Fortune's power to confound even the most virtuous and scrupulous of men, and he was sometimes praised (as in some parts of Shakespeare's *Julius Caesar*) not so much for his republicanism *per se* as for his adherence to older political principles and institutions which he felt to be under threat (see T.R. Langley in *The Yearbook of English Studies*, 6 (1976) 41-52).

2　　　　　*till...grace* i.e. before the birth of Christ. 'Grace', in Christian theology, is the favour of God, freely bestowed on mankind, supremely in the redemptive death of Christ.

24　　　　*idea* Cowley alludes to the Platonic notion of a realm of purely intellectual 'forms' or 'ideas', of which the objects of the everyday world are inferior copies.

　　　　　brave splendid, excellent

42　　　　*Nero's parricide* Nero had his mother Agrippina murdered in A.D. 59.

46　　　　Caesar was said to have staged a scene in which he 'refused' a crown 'offered' to him by Antony.

49　　　　*sprite* ghost. Caesar's ghost was said to have appeared to Brutus before the battle of Philippi.

53-4　　　(alluding to the common superstition that lights burn dim or blue in the presence of ghosts or evil spirits)

77　　　　*generous* noble

(p. 23) *To Mr Hobbes* (1656) Thomas Hobbes (1588-1679), the leading English political philosopher of the mid-seventeenth century, was a royalist and, like Cowley, lived in exile in France during the Interregnum. His most famous work, *Leviathan* (1651), is a comprehensive treatise on human nature, sovereignty, political obligation, and natural law.

16　　　　*emptiness* a vacuum

17　　　　*Stagirite* 'Aristotle, from the town of Stagira, where he was born' (C).

19　　　　'outlasted the Grecian empire, which in the visions of Daniel [7:6] is represented by a leopard, with four wings upon the back, and four heads' (C)

20　　　　'was received even beyond the bounds of the Roman empire, and outlived it' (C)

22　　　　*Mecca* birthplace of Mahomet. Aristotle's works were widely revered in the early Islamic world.

	in spite of Máhomet Mahomet's teaching 'being adapted to the barbarous humour of those people he had first to deal withal, and aiming only at greatness of empire by the sword, forbids all the studies of learning' (C).
23	*a wild deluge* 'the inundation of the Turks, and other nations' (C)
29	*in the schoolmen's hands* in the hands of medieval scholastic philosophers who, according to Cowley, reduced Aristotle's teaching to logic-chopping and arid verbal hair-splitting
39	*want* lack
43	*vain* futile, ineffective
44	*fond* foolish
	dividing wands 'A dividing wand is a two-forked branch of an hazel tree, which is used for the finding out either of veins, or hidden treasures of gold and silver' (C).
49	'All the navigation of the ancients was in these seas' (C).
	The...Euxine the Black Sea
52	*wit* intelligence
59	*only* merely
60	*rudely* in a rough, unfinished state
68	*stuff* material (for clothing)
70	*the shield* (forged, with magnificent engraving, by Vulcan for Aeneas, at the request of Venus, in Virgil's *Aeneid* (8.600-731))
82	*yet* still

(p. 26) ***On the Death of Mr William Hervey*** (1656) William Hervey of Ickworth, Suffolk, entered Pembroke College, Cambridge in 1636, aged 17, and was an undergraduate friend of Cowley. He died at Cambridge in May 1642.

Epigraph	'To the outstandingly gifted, life is short, and old age comes rarely' (Martial, *Epigrams* 6.29.7)
17	(echoing David's lament for Absalom in 2 *Samuel* 18:33)
26	*influ'ence* flowing of stellar fluid or energy, affecting men's destiny (astrological)
35	*the Ledaean stars* Castor and Pollux (the Dioscuri), twin sons of Zeus and Leda, renowned for their fraternal affection, and stellified as the constellation Gemini
37	*toys* frivolities
65	*bays* laurels
66	*contemn* scorn

72   *him* Cyparissus, a youth beloved of Phoebus Apollo, who, having accidentally killed his favourite stag, begged to be allowed to mourn for ever; he was transformed into a cypress tree, thus becoming perpetually associated with graves and lamentation (Ovid, *Metamorphoses* 10.106-42).

114   *in history* in telling them

119   *the first and highest sphere* the outermost of the transparent, concentric spheres which, in the medieval modification of the Ptolomaic astronomical system, was thought to revolve round the earth every twenty four hours, carrying the contained spheres with it, and with them the heavenly bodies

123   *Still* always

149   *rehearse* sing

(p. 31) *On the Death of Mr Crashaw* (1656) On Cowley and the poet Richard Crashaw, see Introduction, p. xxvii.

5   (like the Israelites during their sojourn in Egypt)

7   *spells and charms* During Moses' and Aaron's attempts to free the Israelites, the 'wise men and sorcerers' of Egypt performed conjuring tricks which seemed to duplicate the godly miracles performed by Moses and Aaron, thus causing Pharaoh to harden his heart against the Israelites' release (*Exodus* 7-8).

        withstand stand in the way, hinder

17   *numbers* poetry

20   *calves at Bethel* the two golden calves set up at Bethel and Dan by the sinful King Jeroboam, and worshipped by the children of Israel (1 *Kings* 12)

21   *Pan's death* The death of Pan, the Greek god of flocks and shepherds, was supposed to have coincided with the birth of Christ, when the oracles of pagan antiquity were also supposed to have ceased; Cowley suggests, however, that Apollo continued his activities by inspiring amatory poetry.

26   *we lost it* (by Eve's eating the fruit of the tree of knowledge)

28   *fabulous* given to narrating fantastic stories

30   *she* Crashaw's Muse, who devoted herself to sacred rather than amatory subjects, and thus is imagined as having given birth, like Mary, in a virginal state

34	*But* only
42	*fever* Crashaw died of a fever shortly after taking up his post at Loreto.
43	*the famed chapel* The Santa Casa was the reputed home of the Virgin Mary at Nazareth, which was said to have been miraculously transported by angels to Loreto.
47	*my mother Church* the Church of England
48	*went* (when Crashaw became a Roman Catholic)
55	*nice tenents* precise points of doctrine
57	Cowley is possibly alluding to unsuccessful attempts by members of the court circle to convert him to Roman Catholicism during his time in Paris.
60	*poets militant* The phrase 'the church militant' was used to signify Christians still on earth (the 'church triumphant' denoting those in heaven).
66	*like Elijah* The prophet Elijah ascended by a whirlwind into heaven (2 *Kings* 2:11); his successor Elisha had asked that a 'double portion' of Elijah's spirit might be 'upon' him (ibid., 2:9).

(p. 33) *Ode upon Dr Harvey (1663)* William Harvey (1578-1657), physician to James I and Charles I, was chiefly renowned for his discovery of the circulation of the blood, published in 1628. He had also investigated the growth of the embryo and the incubation of the egg. He was conducting medical experiments in Oxford during Cowley's stay there in the early 1640s.

6	*like Daphne* Daphne, fleeing the amorous advances of Apollo, was metamorphosed into a laurel tree, which was then adopted by the god as his favourite.
12	*eye-beam's point* According to one seventeenth-century theory of sight, objects were seen by 'extramission' (beams projected from the eye on to the object).
	want lack
17	*takes a flood* takes to a river (to escape)
19	*Meander* winding river (here, complex system of blood vessels)
21	*at a bay* cornered, and turning to face her pursuer
28	*a wall* (dividing the right auricle and ventricle from the left)
33	*Proteus* the 'old man of the sea', who could metamorphose himself at will into various guises to elude his pursuers

34	*descried* revealed, made known
35	*wit* intelligence
57	*comments* commentaries (like those on God's other 'book', the Bible)
59	*art* established science
63	*fantastic* (i) fabulous (ii) mad (iii) delusory
68	*Physic* medicine
76	*rage* madness; Harvey published nothing substantial after his treatise on the conception of animals (1651).
78	*the golden fleece* (brought back by Jason and the Argonauts to Greece from Colchis)
85	*Paul's* The old St Paul's Cathedral had so far decayed by the time of James I that Inigo Jones was commissioned to institute a substantial programme of restorations and additions. The fabric, however, continued to deteriorate. Sir Christopher Wren had already been asked to prepare plans for further renovation before the Great Fire of London (1666) virtually destroyed the whole building.

(p. 37) *The Tree of Knowledge* (1656)

Subtitle	*Dogmatists* theologians who sought knowledge of a kind that was (in Cowley's view) proper to God alone, and who argued by means of obfuscatingly intricate structures of logical reasoning (see ll. 21-2); Cowley's poem was pehaps prompted by the publication, in 1650, of Vol. 4 of *De Theologicis Dogmatibus* by the Jesuit scholar, Dionysius Petavius (1583-1652).
2	*phoenix* of unique beauty and value (like the mythical bird)
4	*Porphyrian tree* a logical classification of substance, in diagrammatic form, deriving from the *Isagoge* of the Neoplatonic philosopher Porphyry (A.D. *c*. 234-*c*. 305), and commonly used in medieval logical texts (here punningly aligned with the tree of knowledge of good and evil in the Garden of Eden (*Genesis* 2:9))
6	*were demonstrative* provided absolutely certain proof
17	*science* knowledge
20	*estate* state, condition
28	*fond* foolish

(p. 38) *Life* (1656)

| Epigraph | 'We begin to die as soon as we are born' (Manilius, *Astronomica* 4.16) |

89

7	*bait* stop for refreshment
10-13	Cowley alludes to the belief that angels, though able to understand human language and to use it when communicating with human beings, obtain their own knowledge not by abstracting it from sensations, or by making judgements in language, but through an intuitive knowledge of essences given to them directly by God (see St Thomas Aquinas, *Summa Theologica* 1a, q. 57, art. 1; q. 58, art. 4).
10	Cowley notes that Plato's belief that 'nothing truly is but God' was approved by the church fathers, but excepts angels, on the grounds that they do not partake in the 'perpetual flux of being' that is the human lot.
13	*speak things* Cowley notes that in classical literature and in the Bible, 'the gods' frequently 'call things by other names than we do'.
14	*figure* (of speech)
24	*has no space* i.e. in the eyes of God (Cowley's note refers to *Isaiah* 40:15)
30	*hieroglyphic proofs* ('because heraldry consists of figures of beasts, stars, flowers, and such like, as the hieroglyphics did of the ancient Egyptians' (C))
33	*twenty thousand years* Cowley's note points out that the Egyptians' chronology was impressionistic and contradictory, partly because of 'the equivocal term of the year among them'.
34	*maravedies* small Spanish coins
44	*Mathusalem* Methuselah, the patriarch of *Genesis* 5:27, who was said to have lived 'nine hundred sixty and nine years'.
46	*the womb* i.e. life, death being here imagined as the 'birth' of the soul into a better existence

(p. 40) ***Against Hope*** (first published in Crashaw's *Steps to the Temple* (1646), where its stanzas alternate with Crashaw's poem 'On Hope'; reprinted, *1647, 1656*)

2	*Alike* equally
	miss fail
4	*horns* alternatives (each of which are equally unfavourable)
12	*but* only
14	*clogging* burdening, encumbering

18	*custom* tax, duty
19	*close* sealed
20	*its* the *1668* reading; 'his' in *1647* and *1656*.
22	*blanks* lottery tickets with no prize
24	*still* always
	or...or either...or
28	*presently* immediately
30	*ignes fatui* will-o'-the-wisps (phosphorescent lights which hover over marshy ground)
34	*chemics'* alchemists'
36	*'Anon!'* 'Soon!' The alchemists/lovers are led on by the hope that they will shortly attain their desires.

(p. 41) *For Hope* (*1647*; reprinted, *1656*)

5	*manna* the miraculous food provided by God for the Israelites in the desert (*Exodus* 16:15-35)
6	*sev'ral* individual
7	*sure-entailed* bequeathed in such a way that the settlement is securely fixed
8	*alienate* transfer to someone else's ownership
13	*prepar'ative* medicine which prepares the body to receive a particular course of treatment
17	*earnest-money* deposit, pledge
24	*portion* inheritance
	moveables personal property
32	*way* (used frequently of the Christian religion)
	end (used frequently of Christ)

(p. 43) *To the New Year* (*1656*)

1	*Janus* 'Janus was the god to whom the year was dedicated, and therefore it began with his festival, and the first month was denominated from him; for which cause he was represented with two faces, to show that he looked both backward upon the time past, and forward upon the time to come; and sometimes with four faces, to signify (perhaps – for I know other reasons are given) the four seasons of the year' (C).
7	The temple of Janus was shut in times of peace, and 'opened again with great ceremony' (C) when a war broke out.
21	*lees* dregs
57	*character* alphabet, writing symbols

58   *the Book of Fate* According to Ovid (*Metamorphoses* 15.808-
            15), the Fates record the destinies of all men and women
            on indestructible tablets of brass and iron.

(p. 45) *Seneca, from 'Thyestes'* (*1668**, in the essay 'Of Obscurity') Cowley
translates *Thyestes* 391-403.

4   *giddy* bewildering
18   *'scutcheon* commemorative coat of arms

(p. 46) *Horace : Book 3, Ode 1* (*1668**, in the essay 'Of Greatness')
2   *the great vulgar* the large mass of people
23   *Damocles* Damocles praised the tyrant Dionysius of
            Syracuse as the happiest of men. He was invited by
            Dionysius to a banquet, at which he found a sword sus-
            pended over his head by a single horse-hair.
36   *halcyon* During the mating of the halcyons (sea-birds)
            on their floating nest, the winds and waves were said to
            become calm.
45   *evil aspects* times when the stars are in inauspicious
            positions (astrological)
49   The conjunction of Mars (planet of war) and Saturn
            (planet of pestilence and calamity) in the same degree of
            the zodiac was thought to portend disaster.
51   *So* If only
            Jupiter a beneficent planet; those born under it were
            known as 'jovial'. Cowley advocates the cultivation of an
            inner 'joviality'.
59   *wanton* ludicrously extravagant

(p. 48) *'Begin'* (*1668**, in the essay 'The Danger of Procrastination') This
untitled fragment is a translation of Horace, *Epistles* 1.2.40-3.

(p. 48) *'Hell', from the 'Davideis', Book 1* (*1656**) An earlier version of this
passage had formed part of Book 2 of *The Civil War*.
5-10   'That the matter of winds is an exhalation arising out of
            the concavities of the earth, is the opinion of Aristotle,
            and almost all philosophers since him...In those con-
            cavities, when the exhalations...overcharge the place,
            the moist ones turn into water, and the dry ones into
            winds' (C).
8   *th' eternal...waves* 'To give a probable reason of the
            perpetual supply of waters to fountains and rivers, it is

necessary to establish an abyss or deep gulf of waters, into which the sea discharges itself, as rivers do into the sea – all which maintain a perpetual circulation of water, like that of blood in a man's body' (C).

12	*does* = 'do', in modern usage
23	*sprites* spirits
24	*Hesper* Hesperus, the evening star

(p. 50) *The Wish* (*1647*; reprinted, *1656*)
21   (omitted in *1656* and *1668*)

(p. 51) *A Translation out of Virgil, 'Georgics', Book 2* (*1663*; reprinted, *1668*, in the essay 'Of Agriculture') The poem is a free translation of *Georgics* 2.458-540.

5	*clients* petitioners (seeking favours or patronage)
6	*channels* passageways
10	*the dear . . . pride* Tyrian purple (an expensive dye)
17	*artless grots* natural grottoes
19	*salute* greet
27	*Astraea* goddess of Justice, said to have been driven from earth by human wickedness at the end of the mythical Golden Age
37	*disease* (i) illness (ii) disturbance, instability
40	possibly a quotation (unidentified)
41-2	i.e. why are winter days so short and winter nights so long?
41	*the chariot* Apollo's chariot (the sun)
44	*spir'its* vital energies, thought to have been produced by the blood
48	*Tempe* a wooded valley in Thessaly
50	*gross effects* palpable phenomena
52	*vainly* fruitlessly
58	*rods* the *fasces*, symbols of republican authority at Rome
65	*gownèd* (a reference to lawyers' gowns)
69	*main* sea
72	*foolish whistlings* vapid sound
	name title
76	*Tyrian beds* beds with draperies of Tyrian purple (see note on l. 10)
80	*their antipodes* the opposite side of the world
92	*Twice dyed* dyed to an unusually deep colour
102	*genius* personal tutelary spirit

103	*sacred shade* shade of a tree dedicated to a rural deity
111	*Sabines* a hardy people who, in early times, inhabited the hilly region east of Rome
112	*Etrurian* Etruscan
113	*Remus...brother* Romulus and Remus were the legendary founders of Rome. Romulus was worshipped as a god after his death.
116	*poor...days* the Golden (Saturnian) Age, in which money was unknown
118	i.e. courted death by shipwreck (?)
122	*to...use* i.e. in sacrifices

(p. 55) *Horace: Epode 2* (1668, in the essay 'Of Agriculture') See Introduction (p. xxiv) on Cowley's omission of the last four lines of Horace's poem.

3	*the...mortals* dwellers in the Golden Age
19	*use* profit, return
25	*careless* free from cares
29	*orgies* revels, celebrations (not pejorative)
34	*sullen Jove* stormy weather (Jove being god of the sky, and thus of the weather)
36	*concert* harmonious sound (of their barking)
38	*toil* net
47	*Sabines* See 'A Translation out of Virgil's *Georgics*', note on l. 112.
48	*Apulia* a region in southern Italy
52	*pin* make secure
	kine cattle
53	*against* until
59	*lustful* aphrodisiac
61	*ortolans* garden buntings (thought a delicacy)
	godwits marsh birds, like curlews (also eaten)

(p. 57) *The Country Mouse: A Paraphrase upon Horace, Book 2, Satire 6* (1663; reprinted, 1668, in the essay 'Of Agriculture') Cowley only renders the last part (ll. 79-117) of Horace's satire, in which, in the course of a mealtime conversation at Horace's Sabine farm, Cervius, the poet's rustic neighbour, is imagined as narrating the homely fable of the two mice in response to another guest's envious remarks about a local miser. In the translation of Horace edited by Alexander Brome (1666), Cowley's version was reprinted and prefixed by an imitation of the first part of Horace's satire by Thomas Sprat which updates Horace's setting to 1662, and in which Cervius is humorously reincarnated as 'C[owley]' (see Harold F. Brooks in *Review of English Studies*, 25 (1949), 129-30).

2	*seated* (i) settled (ii) placed
	commodiously (i) conveniently (ii) comfortably
4	*substantial* (i) moderately wealthy (ii) quite important in his society (iii) burly, portly
5	*the main* his own interests
10	*belighted* stranded in the daylight (the opposite of 'be-nighted')
15	*fitches* small wild peas
	peason peas
18	*hautgoust* piquant relish (pronounced to rhyme with 'August')
19	*swerd* rind
25	*genius* personal tutelary spirit
26	*nice* over-refined
	epicurean See 'The Grasshopper', note on l. 32, and Introduction, pp.xix-xx.
35	*obscure* (i) out-of-the-way (ii) dark
38	*gen'rous* beneficent, noble
53	*Phoebus* Apollo, the Greek sun god
	Thetis' a sea nymph; here almost the goddess of the sea.
54	*blushed* The sea is reddened by the setting sun.
65	*Mortlake's noble loom* Mortlake in Surrey was the site of a famous tapestry factory.
68	*Cynthia's* the moon goddess's
69	*meridies* mid point
83	*wanton* carefree
95	*tares* wild peas, growing as weeds among the corn

(p. 59) *Claudian's Old Man of Verona* (1663; reprinted, 1668, in the essay 'The Dangers of an Honest Man in Much Company') The poem is a translation of the second epigram by the late Roman poet Claudian (d. *c.* A.D. 404).

7	*propension* leaning forward, stooping
15	*change...year* At Rome, the two consuls were elected annually, and events were dated by reference to the consuls currently holding office.
19-20	i.e. he can tell the time of day by the shadows cast by the trees on his land
26	*Benacus' lake* Lake Garda, near Verona
27	*age* generation

(p. 60) *The Complaint* (1663)

1	*intellectual* apprehensible by the mind or imagination (as opposed to the senses)
5	*careful* full of cares
6	*Cam* the river running through Cambridge
13	*figures* (i) shapes (ii) figures of speech
18	*Ismenus* a river in Boeotia (the legendary home of the Muses) near Thebes (close to the birthplace of Pindar)
26	*estate* fortune, possessions
32	*portion* legacy, allotment (of talent)
33	*the mighty Nine* the Muses
48	*cast* reckon, total
52	*apostasy* abandonment of your original allegiances
53	*the public storm* the Civil War and Commonwealth, which ended with the Restoration of Charles II in 1660
69	*old Gideon's miracles* the signs given by God to Gideon, to assure him of the genuineness of his divinely-appointed mission to save Israel. Gideon asked that God should cause the evening dew to fall upon a lamb's fleece while all the ground around it remained dry. Later he asked that the fleece should remain dry while the earth around it was soaked (*Judges* 6:36-40).
72	*quickened* made full of life
76-8	(one of the threats issued by God against the Israelites if they disobeyed His commandments (*Deuteronomy* 28:23))
82-9	Jacob contracted with Laban to have Laban's daughter Rachel as his wife, saying that he would serve seven years for her. On the wedding night, Laban substituted his elder daughter Leah for Rachel. He then promised Jacob the hand of Rachel if he would first marry Leah, then serve a further seven years (*Genesis* 29:1-30). Cowley alludes to his disappointment at not being offered the Mastership of the Savoy after the Restoration (see Principal Dates: 1661, 1663).
99	*manna* See 'For Hope', note on l. 5.
113	*still* always
116	*but* only
	ever always
121	(an allusion to so-called 'fairy rings': patches of rank or withered grass supposedly produced by the dancing of fairies)
127	*reduce* bring back, restore

130	*cross* contrary, blowing across the direct course of a ship
131	*nerves* muscles
140	*Sapphira* Ananias and Sapphira, two early Christians, sold some land and secretly kept back part of the proceeds for themselves. Accused by St Peter of defrauding God, both dropped dead on the spot (*Acts* 5:1-10).

(p. 65) *In Imitation of Martial's Epigram* (1656)

12	*unmixed* pure
24-5	*of which...account* for our responsible use of which we will be held accountable
26	*stay* delay (to do so)

(p. 67) *The Muse* (1656) On this poem, see Introduction, pp. xxi-xxii.

2	*take the air* (i) enjoy an outing (ii) fly
3	*trace* harness
5	*Smooth-paced* Evenly-stepping
8	*postilion* driver (of the first pair of coach-horses)
12	*Figures* (of speech)
	Conceits ingenious analogies
	Raptures 'uncommon heats of imagination' (Johnson, *Dictionary*)
	Sentences epigrams
17	*put on* hurry on
23	*liquid sky* sea
27	*busy* meddling, prying
30	*say* (at the creation)
36	*Thou fathoms't* You penetrate
45	(alluding to the popular belief that the stars control men's fortunes)
46	*close* secret
50	*secondine* the sack within which an embryo develops in the womb
61	*snake* the year (thus represented in Egyptian hieroglyphics)
64	*Thou comfitest* You preserve in sugar
72	*eternity* See Introduction, pp. xxi-xxii.

(p. 69) *The Praise of Pindar* (1656) Cowley imitates ll. 1-32 of Horace's poem.

1	*Pindar* The Greek poet Pindar (518-438 B.C.) was the author of choral odes, many of which celebrated victories

in athletic contests. Cowley's presentation of Pindar as a poet of lofty imagination, bold imagery, sudden digressions and daring transitions was widely influential in the late seventeenth and early eighteenth centuries, though his conception of Pindar as a poet of 'various and irregular' metres was criticised by William Congreve in his 'Discourse on the Pindaric Ode' (1710).

2	*phoenix* unique (like the mythical bird)
3	*Daedalus* the legendary Athenian craftsman who fashioned wings for himself and his son Icarus from feathers and wax; Icarus flew too near the sun, the wax melted, and he fell into the sea, which was subsequently named 'Icarian' after him.
12	*figures* (of rhetoric)
13	*dithyrambic* Pindar's dithyrambs (none of which survive) were antistrophic hymns on mythological themes; here the term suggests 'a bold, free, enthusiastical kind of poetry, as of men, inspired by Bacchus – that is, half drunk' (C).
19	*numbers* verses
24	*at Pisa's race* In early times the Olympic games were held at Pisa in southern Greece.
27	*artful* skilful
37	*The Theban swan* Pindar was born near Thebes.
42	*unballassed* unsteady

(p. 71) *The Resurrection* (1656) The poem was described by Cowley as 'truly pindarical, falling from one thing into another, after his enthusiastical manner [i.e. like a man possessed]'.

8	*it* i.e. virtue
14 .	*well-fitted* harmonious
15	*decently* in fitting order, decorously
20	(alluding to the belief that the 'music of the spheres' will end at the Last Judgement)
26-7	Virgil 'shall see the whole world burnt to ashes like Troy, the destruction of which was so excellently written by him [in *Aeneid*, Book 2], though it was built like Troy, too, by divine hands (the walls of Troy were said to be built by Apollo and Neptune)' (C).
35	*five thousand years* Cowley notes that 'the ordinary, traditional opinion is that the world is to last six thousand years', but says that he 'could not say "sluggards of six

98

thousand years", because some then would be found alive who had not so much slept at all; the next perfect number (and verse will admit of no broken ones) was five thousand'.

| 52 | *allay* temper |
| 54 | *Pegasus* the Muses' winged horse |

(p. 73) Destiny (1656) 'This ode is written upon an extravagant supposition of two angels playing a game at chess; which if they did, the spectators would have reason as much to believe that the pieces moved themselves, as we can have for thinking the same of mankind, when we see them exercise so many and so different actions' (C).

Epigraph	'This too is destined by Fate, that I should expound the rule of Fate' (Manilius, *Astronomica* 4.118)
2	*prodigy* extraordinary happening
4	*unbred* not properly brought up (i.e. unlike human beings)
	ill-organed not furnished with human organs
6	*policy* political know-how
8	*pawn* 'For a pawn being the least of the pieces, if it can get up to such a degree, grows the greatest, and then has both another name and other motions and powers; for it becomes a queen, which it could never have done if it had not been removed, and carried to such an height' (C).
14	*the losing party* (with a glance at the royalists in the Civil War)
16	*the bag* (where captured pieces in the chess game are collected)
17	*mated* put into 'checkmate'
18	*philosophy* science
20	*election* the power to exercise choice
34	*navel* umbilical cord
36	*cov'enant* the engagement with God entered into by believers at baptism
42	*th' Exchange* the building where merchants met for the transaction of business
	Bar lawcourts
46	*doom* fate, destiny
53	*lambent* one that plays gently on material without burning it
55	*influence* (i) power bestowed by Fate (astrological) (ii) influence in the world

99

(p. 75) *Ode: Of Wit* (1656)

2	*Thou* The addressee is unidentified.
3	*the first matter* the primal chaos
8	*spirits* ghosts (who were supposed to appear in bodies of condensed air)
12	*Zeuxis'* The Greek painter Zeuxis was said to have painted grapes so life-like that the birds came to pick at them.
14	*multiplying* magnifying
20	*tit'ular bishops* A 'titular bishop' in the Roman Catholic Church was one whose supposed sphere of jurisdiction actually lay outside the domain of Rome, and was thus merely notional.
23	*florid* elaborate, ornate
30	*the Theban wall* Amphion, a ruler of Thebes in Greek legend, was said to have been a harper of such skill that the stones of the city wall were drawn into place by his music.
37	*Sev'ral* Separate
42	*Dutch men and English boys* (both seen as likely connoisseurs of feeble puns)
44	*acrostics* puzzle-poems in which one or more letters of each line, taken in order, spell a word or group of words
50	*Bajazet* a ranting tyrant in Marlowe's play *Tamburlaine the Great*
51	*tall* high-flown, far-fetched
52	*short-lunged Seneca* The style of the Roman philosopher (*c.* 4 B.C. – A.D. 65) was renowned for its pithy concentration.
61	*forms* Plato's 'ideas' (see 'Brutus', note on l. 25)
64	*mirror* pattern or model; in Cowley's Christian thought, the ideal realm of the Platonic forms is identified with the mirror of truth, in which God sees both Himself and futurity (the two being synonymous, since everything that is or will be derives from Him).

(p. 78) *'The Music of Creation', from the 'Davideis', Book 1* (1656) This self-contained digression prefaces the scene in Cowley's epic where David is called to play before King Saul.

7	*correspondence* (i) congruity (ii) harmony; Cowley plays

throughout on God's dual rôle as creator/maker and poet/musician.

8   *motions* (i) movements (ii) melodic progressions

11-12   Cowley associates the variously-pitched voices in a choir with the elements making up the world.

18   *decent* fitting

20   *science* knowledge, skill

21   *rehearse* recite

23   *world* the universe

28   *sympathy* consonance, harmony